Land's End *- Iohn O'Groats
Self He

First published by Royston Wood (not pictured above)
2012

This 2015 edition is completely revised after two
further end to end rides

Dedication

This book is dedicated to my long suffering wife who has to act as a single parent every time I start planning a cycle challenge. The time I'm away from home on the ride itself is bad enough but then there's the endless weekends of training beforehand. But she needs the training otherwise she won't be hard and lean enough to survive an onslaught of boys for the week I'm away.

Her commitment and contribution is far greater than mine, it's quiet on the bike.

Contents

Introduction

There are a number of books and various websites that give advice, guidance and different routes for getting from one end of the country to the other on what must be Britain's most famous long distance challenge ride.

Which begs the question, "Why should you buy this one?"

In writing this book I have followed one main ethos: I am not an expert on all things cycling.

No – don't give up just yet! This is a layman's guide written by a layman based on his experiences of planning a ride from scratch. It sets out the issues that you will need to consider (preparation, training, equipment, travel to and from the start/finish, route, accommodation, etc..) and is designed to provoke thought in each aspect of your ride rather than try to give you definitive answers.

There are good reasons for this. For a start, things change. Between the time of me typing this and you reading it many 'facts' which could be contained in the book may no longer be correct.

Let me give an example to illustrate the point. When I first tried to plan my ride I checked train times and costs to John O'Groats (more specifically Wick, 16 miles short of John O'Groats). The train left Plymouth about 20:00 and, after three changes, arrived in Wick 18 hours later at roughly 14:00 next day. I can't remember the precise times but it meant I arrived with time to cycle to a B&B near the start, ready to begin in the morning. The cost with bike, booking in advance, was about £75. That ride fell through but the next year I planned again. When I came to book the train I found it had changed. It now took 28 hours with an overnight stop and cost £240 (plus the cost of accommodation for the overnight unless I wanted to spend 8 hours on the platform).

Another example of why I have tried to provoke thought rather than dictate your actions is routing. When I first considered riding an end to end [as all tours between Land's End and John O'Groats will be referred to in this book] finding a route was daunting. I thought the best thing to do would be to find a route somebody else had used. I got hold of several but none of them were really suitable to the journey I wished to make. I soon concluded that routing was a very personal thing and that nobody else's route would ever suit me entirely. The problem was that none of the guides I had purchased actually gave me any advice about how to devise a route myself.

So, whilst I have included a narrative of the journey to give you a flavour of the experience, I am aware that some aspects of it may not appeal to you. Therefore my route section deals with the types of things that you will want to consider when deciding upon your route (such as terrain, how far a day you want to travel, type of accommodation etc..) and how to produce a route with written directions rather than leave you with no option but to use my route.

For your convenience I have divided the book into three main sections, cunningly entitled Beginning, Middle and End. The beginning section deals with the things you will need to consider, well, at the beginning. Ideally you need to have a good idea about these things early on as they will help shape what goes on in the middle – sorting your route and getting the training in. And most of us will have to do these things before the end section, which deals with the ride itself.

So, without more ado...

In this text trips from Land's End to John O'Groats are referred to as LEJOG and from John O'Groats to Land's End as JOGLE. The generic term end-to-end will be used where the context does not require a specific direction. I am hoping to save a lot of typing in this way (but if I keep warbling on about it I might use up any typing time I might have saved).

Beginning

The first thing we need to do is work out what level of assistance you need. To do this read the following statements and see which is most applicable to you:

1. *I am really keen to do an end to end but have no idea where to start.*

    This statement cannot really apply to you because you have already done your most important bit of research and acquired this book. You have a natural instinct to cut to the heart of a problem and find the best solutions (at a very reasonable price). Read on.

2. *I have done some initial research and found a renowned and highly acclaimed book on the subject but don't know what to do next.*

    Put this book down and read that one!

3. *I am really quite lazy and just googled, "The book I am looking for that has all the answers I need to plan and complete that Land's End to John O'Groats [or vice versa] ride I've always talked about doing but never got around to". This book came up so I bought it.*

    Oh well. Never mind. Let's try and make the best of it. Fix yourself a large mug of tea/coffee/beer/gin, settle yourself in a comfy chair and get someone to read this book to you.

Better still, get someone to précis it and tell you the bits you need to know. This will save you a lot of time. Don't let them annotate or deface the book itself though (notes on paper or dictation device would be best) because this will have a disastrous effect on the resale value of this ([possibly] soon to be) highly sought after text. If you are lucky enough to have secured a 1st edition copy you may want to consider keeping it in dust free environment, away from damp and direct sunlight, and increasing your home contents insurance. Early copies have been known to fetch nearly 10% of their original price on a well-known online auction site.

Why do you want to do that?

Be prepared to face this question. It is either something people get – or not. And the trouble is it isn't always very easy to answer if they don't get it.

For most people that do it, long distance cycling is about facing a challenge of endurance and endeavour. Of course, each individual has a mix of other stuff that they get out of it, but at the core is that feeling of satisfaction, of a job well done, on reaching the end.

And at the end, in that warm glow of achievement, we forget the pain and suffering we have endured during the course of the ride. Those swear words that bounced around our heads halfway up that 20% climb have faded away. We have forgotten our pledge, 'never to do this #@⚑☀ ride again', whilst battling against horizontal hail in the teeth of a 40mph headwind. We are left only with good memories, even if that good memory is, 'It was a pig of a ride but I finished!' [and if only 10% of the starters did, even better].

The point is, we can't remember pain. Yes, we can remember that we suffered pain but we cannot actually relive it. So the memory of the pain is weak and soon subsumed.

By way of illustration I can point to my own experiences on my end to end. In the aftermath of my ride I was left with the overall feeling that it went much better than I anticipated and was, on the whole, much easier than I thought it would be. I had ridden steadily each day with a fairly constant energy level and had not suffered much at any point on the ride. I knew a couple of stretches had been tricky but nothing to have gotten me down.

What I wasn't aware of is the fact that my wife had been typing up all the text messages I had been sending her (I sent one every two hours or so to show I was still alive) and converting them to blog like emails to send to my work colleagues and sponsors to show how things were going. And they were copied verbatim.

I was most surprised to find words like, 'strain' and 'sick' and 'tired' and 'hard' and 'crap' in my texts. And they also reminded me that I had felt so bad on day two that I had decided to cut out my slight side detour over the Kirkstone Pass (which was to be a highlight challenge) because I was worried it would rekindle the sciatica in my right leg.

The thing is, even with the reality spelt out in black and white before me, I still can't quite conjure up the memories to go with the texts. It is all very positive in my memory and that is why I would have no hesitations in doing it all again.

But that can be hard to explain to somebody who can't grasp the concept, perhaps because they have never challenged their body and mind in that way. So, if you get fed up with trying to explain why you are doing it, then do the ride for charity. Everyone understands that.

Planning

The critical thing about planning is to start doing it. Until you get the ball rolling your end to end will not progress beyond the, 'ride I've always talked about' stage. I've found the best way to kick off is to set a date. When you put a cross on the calendar it tends to focus the mind. It works even better if you tell other people about it because it's much harder to back out or let the date slide.

Of course there will be a number of factors for you to think about before randomly sticking a pin in the calendar:

- preferred weather conditions. Do you want to be battling through snow? Are you uncomfortable riding in the heat?

- hours of daylight - how long do you intend to ride each day?

- type and cost of accommodation – high or low season.

- sights you want to see – maybe you want to see snow on the hills or the highlands in heather or daffodils in Windermere or cones on the road or caravans blocking every lane.

- personal matters. Things specific to you that will constrain when you can do the ride such as work, prior commitments, family matters etc.

Once you have a date set (or at least pencilled in) you can start planning your activities. To illustrate this I have set out below how I set about planning my trip.

After months of dithering I started actually 'planning' over the Christmas break. Initially this involved picking a date [after due consultation process with spouse – highly recommended] and marking it on the calendar.

In arriving at the date the things I took into consideration were:

- I wanted to complete the ride in 6 days and guestimated I would need to cycle about 150 mile a day. At my normal average speeds over this distance I thought I would need 12 hours in the saddle plus stopping time. So I would need to have plenty of daylight or be prepared to ride in the dark. The beginning of May to Middle of August would be good.

- I like riding in warm sunny conditions so to maximize the possibility of this I narrowed down my time window to July and August.

- My wife would be left to deal with the household of two small boys, two puppies and two cats whilst working herself, so to give her a fair chance I had to avoid school holidays. This ruled out the last week of July and all of August.

- I was riding solo and wanted to keep my equipment down so did not want to camp. I decided to use B&B accommodation but my budget was tight so I had to avoid peak season. This meant as far from the summer holidays as possible so early July seemed to be the best bet.

- I wanted to start on a Sunday to give me Saturday for travel to the start and the following Saturday and Sunday for recovery [in hind sight – ha bloody ha!] before going back to work on the Monday. So my date was set as the first Sunday in July.

Having set the date a number of things

Top tip:

Plan how you are going to get to the start early on because it may impact on your other plans.

immediately crystalised:

- I had a date for travel and could begin searching for the costs of various options for travelling to John O'Groats.

- I knew how long I had before the ride for training so could set an appropriate training schedule.

- I also knew how long I had to lose those extra kilos that I didn't want to haul from one end of the country to the other.

- I had a time frame to set a budget to cover the expenses of the trip.

How am I going to get to the start/from the /finish?

This is not always the first thing people think about when planning their ride but I would suggest putting it early in the planning stage for two reasons:

1. I didn't and ended up with problems (see below).

2. Having fixed (and probably paid for) your travel, you have another incentive to do the ride.

There are a number of options for travelling to/from Land's End and John O'Groats:

Train

This is the preferred option of many. Trains are available as close to John O'Groats as Wick (approx 16 miles) or Thurso (approx 15 miles) and as close to

Land's End as Penzance (approx 10 miles). You can cycle/taxi the intervening distance.

Depending on your start point you may have to make a number of train changes. You will probably need at least one train to Edinburgh then it's a change there to Inverness where there is a final change to Wick/Thurso. [Make sure you book a space on the train for your bike in advance because these are very limited.]

However, before assuming this is the best way to go check the train times and costs well in advance because they vary over time! As a cautionary tale, I originally planned a JOGLE for the year before I eventually did it [I didn't put a cross on the calendar and let it all slide]. I had investigated the various ways of getting to John O'Groats and the train was perfect. I could leave from Plymouth on Friday evening on a sleeper train and arrive in Wick mid-afternoon on Saturday. This left plenty of time to cycle to my selected B&B near the start for a good night's rest before the start on Sunday. The cost, if I booked in advance, was £69 plus £3 to book my bike. Sorted.

The next year I assumed all would be the same. However, when I came to make my booking (having already booked several of my B&B stops on my route to Land's End) I found the time table and costs had changed dramatically. The train journey was now considerably longer with an overnight stop instead of a sleeper train. Aside from the inconvenience and cost of an extra night's accommodation, I would need to take an extra day's holiday to cover the additional day lost travelling. And the cost had gone up to £240, even booking in advance. So I ended up chasing around trying to find a better way.

Car

If you are lucky (like me) you might live within an easy car drive of one or the other. I live within a three hour drive of Land's End. If you are blessed (like me) with a loving and tolerant spouse you might be able to persuade them to drop you off/pick you up.

If you are not blessed, or even lucky, you can still hire a car one way to the start/from the finish. At least that's what a number of guides suggest.

Having found that the train was going to put a sizable dent in my budget and time arrangements I investigated car hire as an alternative. I discovered that the closest place to Land's End that you can drop a hire car off is in Penzance – which is ok, only ten miles of so away. If you don't want to cycle an extra 10 mile [shame on you – although it is unfairly hilly if you've done the JOGLE] you can get a taxi.

But the closest drop off for one way hire that I could find to John O'Groats was Inverness, about 100 miles short. Options to/from there were to cycle all the way or take the train between Inverness and Wick and taxi or cycle the 16 miles or so between Wick and John O'Groats. If your budget is not limited you could get a taxi from Inverness to John O'Groats.

Bearing in mind the 10-11 hour drive from Devon all the way up to Inverness and the petrol costs plus the train connections and need for an extra night's accommodation, the cost and time implications seemed to be as bad or worse than the train.

Plane

Finding both the train and car hire expensive and time consuming I turned, almost in desperation, to air travel.

The closest airport to Land's End offering internal connections with the rest of the UK is in Newquay (approx. 40 miles). The closest to John' O'Groats is Wick (approx. 20 miles). The normal taxi/cycle options to/from apply.

I was surprised to find that I could travel from

Plymouth to Wick (via Edinburgh) for about £100. And it would only take about 5 hours including the stopover. So, much cheaper and much quicker than the train or car hire. The only downside was that I could only take my bike as standby luggage. Which meant I might arrive at the airport and be told my bike could not travel. Which would be a problem.

So I investigated posting my bike to Wick. I googled bike shops in Wick and contacted one to ask whether they would be willing to accept delivery of my bike. When they agreed I tried googling bike postal to Wick. Unfortunately all of the operatives I could find on-line wanted to charge an enormous sum to take my bike to the Highlands. In the end I picked up the yellow pages and found a local courier who would ship it for £25.00. By lucky coincidence the franchise was owned by the same people who owned my local bike shop and was housed in the same building. So when the time came to send my bike on its way I dropped it into the bike shop for a full service and they packed it for me and took it next door ready to be whizzed to Wick. Ideal.

Well, almost. Unfortunately there were no flights from Edinburgh to Wick on a Saturday so I had to travel on Friday. Whilst this meant I had to take an extra day off work, which was no real hardship, it also meant that the B&Bs I had booked were now all a day too late! So I had to frantically ring around and re-book – thankfully with no difficulty. And on the positive side I would be starting, and hence finishing, a day earlier so I would have an extra day to recover at the end.

Coach

A final option for travel is by coach. Again, the closest you can get to Land's End is Penzance and for John O'Groats it's Wick. National Express have a fairly wide ranging network throughout England and to Edinburgh. From there up it's City Link [bus/coach company, not parcel courier!].

Please note that whilst you can take your bike as luggage [check this before you book because things change] you will need to package it.

Whilst the coach can be relatively cheap it is also slow, so be prepared for a long journey.

Where am I going to sleep on my route?

There are many different types of accommodation you can stay at during your tour. And in most parts of the country you will have plenty of choice:

- tent – This is probably the cheapest form of accommodation but does mean carrying extra stuff. You should consider the availability of sites, especially in peak season, and whether they will allow single night stays. If you are intending to do a spot of guerilla camping behind the nearest sheltered hedge, make sure you check for the presence of cows – and bulls – before pitching!

- B&B – If your budget is tight it is worth organizing this in advance, even if this only means taking a list of the cheaper ones at strategic points on your route, because prices and standards very enormously (and not always proportionately!). I booked ahead and found the cheapest in each area and even then I had a range of £19 - £35 (2009). And note that whilst the second B - breakfast - is a very useful thing to the long distance cyclist it's not much use if you are up and gone before breakfast is served!

- motels – These are convenient, especially if you are doing a main road route. They're also good if you like your anonymity and don't want to spend half an hour at the end of a tiring day chatting to a B&B owner about what you are doing. They tend to be more expensive than B&Bs though.

- hotels – Get you! This is meant to be a challenge you know. I hope you oversleep in that comfortable bed and have to ride double hard to catch up.
- youth hostels – Not as cheap as they used to be. But then, not so full of youths either.
- park bench - The best ones are highly sought after so you may have to plan to arrive early enough to stake your claim, which could curtail your mileage.
- gutter - Some thought should be given to this in advance as not all gutters are overly conducive to restful sleep. For instance, you might like to avoid gutters outside pubs and night clubs [unless you really can't stagger any further from the door]. If it's raining anchor yourself down with some ballast otherwise you may wake up some distance from where you started, which can be disorientating. The advantages of gutter accommodation are that: it is cheap, you don't have to detour from your route to get to it, other guests won't turn their noses up at your scruffy, sweaty appearance, there are no queues for the toilet and the heater won't be stuck on all night with the window painted shut. On the down side: security is a risk, there is a chance of being squashed in the night by passing lorries and you might get eaten by foxes. Also, in some areas, spaces are limited, especially at peak times – you try finding a free gutter space in Glasgow at 3:00am on a Saturday morning.

All of that is assuming that you intend to sleep at all. You might not need to if you're hard.

What will I need to take with me on my ride?

Basically:

- bike [minimum requirement]
- stuff to put on bike
- bags
- stuff to put in bags
- clothes

Bike

This is fairly fundamental! The end to end has been completed on just about any kind of bike you can think of so don't feel restricted in your choice.

Of course, for most of us the choice may be limited to the bike we have. But if you have a number of bikes to choose from or are looking to buy a new bike for the trip (it's a good excuse) I have listed the main types of bike below with a few pros and cons for each.

Please note that if you are looking to reward yourself with a new bike for the trip:

1. Bear in mind your proposed use for it after the tour. For example you may decide a road bike is the best for the tour but if you want to do mainly off road afterwards it won't be much use to you.

2. Buy it well in advance so you can get used to it on your training rides.

3. My summary of bike characteristics is made in the broadest of terms [and is not necessarily very impartial]. Within each category you will find a baffling array of options leaving you balancing perceived benefits and costs from one bike to another. For instance a road racing bike could cost you anything from a few hundred pounds up to several thousand depending on the build quality, weight and performance of the frame, gears, wheels and other components.

Road racing bike

Designed for racing on solid road surfaces, these bikes are light weight and responsive with an aggressive frame geometry built to maximise aerodynamics, not  comfort. They have high gearing to maximize speed.

They have restricted loading capacies without attachment points for racks etc. It is often difficult or impossible to fit full mudguards and tyre size is limited due to lack of clearance between the wheel and the frame.

They can feel unwieldy with the back and front loaded (which, whilst difficult, is possible).

It is not surprising that the end-to-end 'normal' bike record was set on a racing bike (fully supported so no need to carry anything other than a water bottle).

Pros	Cons
• light weight • responsive • fast • gives impression you mean business • uncomfortable enough to make dropping off to sleep unlikely	• can feel unwieldy when loaded • restricted loading capabilities • uncomfortable for long distances • high gearing may be tiring at the end of each day

end-to-end record:

1 day, 20 hours, 4 minutes and 20 seconds for men
2 days, 4 hours, 45 minutes and 11 seconds for women

Road touring bike

Designed for touring on solid road surfaces. These bikes look very similar to racing bikes but have a frame geometry built more for comfort than aerodynamics.

They are stronger, and hence heavier, than racing bikes being designed to carry loads. They have mounting positions for racks and mudguards and generally have wider wheels accommodating fatter more comfortable (but slower and more energy draining) tyres. They have a wide range of gears, some very low for slogging up hills fully laden.

Pros	Cons
• more comfortable over long distances • can carry heavy loads • wide range of gears	• heavier than a racing bike • fatter tyres cause greater rolling resistance

end-to-end record:

There is no specific end-to-end record for a touring bike

Mountain bike

Designed for use off road.

These bikes have a low centre of gravity making handling easier. And being designed for off road use they offer the opportunity for more adventurous routing and off road detours. They also have some very low gears that can come in handy on steeper sections, especially towards the end of the day when your energy levels are flagging.

However, to deal with off road conditions they are built to be robust and therefore tend to be heavy. Their tyres are considerably wider than those of a road bike and even after fitting slicks they have a much greater rolling resistance (more friction between the tyre and the road). They are therefore less efficient than road bikes, a factor that you will certainly feel in your legs over a long tour. Despite a more relaxed riding position most people find mountain bikes uncomfortable to ride over long distances.

Pros	Cons
<ul><li>easy handling</li><li>ability to do off road routing</li><li>lower gears for hills at end of day</li></ul>	<ul><li>heavy and inefficient</li><li>uncomfortable over long distances</li></ul>

end-to-end record:

There is no specific end-to-end record for mountain bikes.

Hybrid/Urban Cycle

Designed to be somewhere between the mountain bike and the road bike this has more comfort than the road bike and a good spread of gears from high to low. Weight and rolling resistance are somewhere between the two (on like for like cost machines). They offer a compromise between the pros and cons of road and mountain bikes. They are designed with a commuter and occasional weekend use market in mind.

Pros	Cons
• Wide range of gears • more comfortable riding position • mounting points for racks, etc.	• heavy • a compromise of good and bad features

end-to-end record:

There is no specific end-to-end record for hybrid/urban cycles.

Recumbent

These bikes have a completely different seating position to a traditional upright bike. The rider is seated low to the ground with the legs stretching in front. This gives the bike a number of positive  advantages including a low centre of gravity, low frontal area so less wind resistance and a more comfortable seating position. The fact that you are low to the ground is also touted as a safety feature because you have less distance to fall when you are knocked off your bike. [Personally I don't think this would reassure me much as the juggernaut's wheel bore down on me at eye level, about to grind me into the tarmac].

Because of their low frontal area recumbents are fast, as proven by the end-to-end record.

However, they take a lot of practice to get used to. Balance is more difficult and they are a different beast going uphill because you cannot stand on the pedals. I've also been down plenty of cycle paths with barriers that would be impassable for a recumbent. Not sure how you jump kerbs, pot holes or other obstructions either!

Being of a specialist nature you may find it difficult to find spares for a recumbent whilst on tour.

Pros	Cons
• efficient • fast • good added interest for fund raising	• dangerous [?] • difficult to find spares en route • weight
end-to-end record: 1 day, 17 hours, 2 minutes	

Penny farthing

No gears, solid rubber tyres and made out of roughly beaten iron girders. If you have a head for height they are much faster than those old fashioned bone shakers.

Actually you can now buy new penny farthings with pneumatic tyres and brakes for about £500.

Amazingly the record (see below) was set in 1886 and is entirely impressive, especially if you consider the state of the road back then and the fact that the shortest route was much longer because there were fewer bridges. So if you want to break a record this might be the one to go for. Of course you might break your neck instead.

Pros	Cons
• nice view • good added interest for fund raising	• bloody dangerous • bloody uncomfortable • no bloody gears

end-to-end record:

- 5 day and 1 hour – impressive!

Unicycle

Rather you than me.

Pros	Cons
• good added interest for fund raising	• probably spend more time on your back than on your wheel • 50% less likely to get a puncture

end-to-end record:

- 14 days, 12 hours and 41 minutes

Tricycle

Or you could ride a big boy bike with stabilisers.

Pros	Cons
• Great if you want to be the youngest end to end rider – currently 7 years and 9 months (took 22 days) – and haven't mastered a proper bike yet	• 50% more likely to get a puncture

end-to-end record:

- 2 days, 5 hours, 29 minutes and 1 second – not bad for a toddler

Stuff to put on bike

Once you have a bike sorted you need to equip it with a few fundamentals for the trip. There are all sorts of bits and pieces you can buy to stick on your bike but a minimum list for a trip like this is:

- Bike computer
- Bottles
- Pump
- Tyres
- Lights
- Bag(s)

Bike computer

This is a fairly essential piece of kit if you are following a written route of the 'turn left after 1 mile' variety. You might get away without one if you are purely following a map. But even then it's nice to know how far you have gone.

Personally I find a bike computer essential to help me calculate how far I have been, how far I have to go and how long it will take me to get there. Mine also has a heart rate monitor so I can keep an eye on how hard I am working. I have a tendency to push too hard and need to make sure my heart rate doesn't creep up too high for too long. It's not a problem over a short training ride but on day long rides it means I run out of energy before the end.

For the trip I also purchased a satellite navigation device ('sat nav') for the bike. In fact my wife insisted when I said I wasn't taking any maps because they were too bulky. It would have been a very useful aid if:

1. I had remembered to load my route onto it before I left! [I managed to download it via the computer at my overnight B&B near John O'Groats].

2. The built in rechargeable battery lasted longer than 8-9 hours. My average day was 10-12 hours cycling.

3. I had worked out how to use it properly before I started the trip.

If are foolish enough to risk travelling without a map, like me, and you don't have a sat nav, a more basic bit of equipment that might be useful is a compass. If you do get lost it's better to know you are at least heading in vaguely the right direction (until you can find signs to a town you recognise on your route) rather than charging off in a random direction.

Pump

Even if you manage to do the trip without a puncture it is likely that you'll have to put some pressure back into your tyres after several hundred miles of cycling, possibly with a heavy load. And with that in mind you will need a pump that can achieve a reasonably high pressure.

There are a multitude of pumps on the market ranging from co2 gas fired ones to mini pumps to stand pumps. The stand pump is ideal for home because it can achieve a very high pressure with the minimum of effort. It's a bit bulky for the bike though.

Having said that, I was very concerned about being stuck in the middle of nowhere and not being able to put enough pressure in my tyres if I got a puncture, especially with the extra weight on the bike. So I searched the internet and found a mini stand pump, which could achieve high pressure, albeit with a little more effort than a normal stand pump. It was also very reasonably priced at less than £15. The only downside is that it is a very tight fit on the bike. If I don't put it on in a certain way the pedals knock against it. The first few times I used it, it took me longer to get the pump back on the bike than to fix the puncture.

There are many mini pumps on the market that claim to be able to achieve a very high pressure. I'm sure that some of them do. I know that some of them don't because I've had them - and discarded them. One that does is the Lezyne Road Drive Mini Pump. It is a little expensive but it is a thing of simplistic, precision engineering beauty that is lightweight and does the job it is supposed to. This would be the pump I would take with me if I were to do an end to end now.

Another good and reasonably priced option is the traditional, full length, frame fitting pump. But not all frames will accommodate them, such as mine!

Bottles

I would strongly recommend that you take at least 2 x 750ml water bottles (preferably 900ml [1000ml are available but don't fit in a bottle cage very well]).

In 'normal' cycling conditions you will need to drink about 500ml (roughly a pint) of liquid every hour. You can double that if it is hot and/or you are working hard. You might feel you can get away with less but you will suffer for it on a long trip (see section on hydration).

So if it is hot, your 2 x 900ml bottles will last you about 2 hours. If you were carrying only 500ml bottles you would need to fill up every hour. Whilst you might be happy to stop every hour there are certain sections of the trip where it may take you longer than that to get between potential safe watering points. And if you are using a major road route, like mine, there are very few watering points because the roads bypass all the towns. So to avoid having to make regular detours you need to make sure you are carrying a reasonable supply of liquids.

Tyres

The main features you are looking for in a tyre are:

- puncture resistance – many tyres now have a puncture resistant layer beneath the rubber. These can make a considerable difference to the number of punctures you get. In the year of my end to end I cycled about 9,000 miles on these tyres and suffered 3 punctures (none on the end to end itself). Of those, two were caused by nails, which no amount of armouring would have stopped.

- grip in wet weather – some rubber compounds and tread patterns are more grippy in wet, muddy conditions than others. A slick racing tyre will not offer the same sure grip as a heavily threaded mountain bike tyre.

- rolling resistance – this is how much energy is lost through friction between the tyre and the road surface. Generally the smoother the thread and the narrower the tyre the less the rolling resistance will be. Hence slick 19mm racing tyres will have low rolling resistance and take less effort to ride on.

- weight – the heavier the tyre the more weight you have to carry across the country.

- comfort – the thicker the tyre the more suspension there is between you and the road surface, hence the more comfortable the ride. A 19mm racing tyre, pumped to 120psi, does not offer ultimate comfort!

As you can see some factors are almost the opposite of others and you will have to balance up what is important to you and your ride. There are tyres whose manufacturers claim they offer everything, but then so would I if I was trying to sell one.

The life expectancy of tyres varies enormously but I would expect one to last about 2,000 miles. So check them for wear before you go – you have about 1,000 miles to cover and don't really want to have to change them half way. I put new tyres on my bike (Continental Ultra Gatorskin 25mmx700mm – couldn't get anything fatter due to lack of frame clearance) before the start and then put the old ones back on once those were past their useful life.

Lights

Basically there are two types of light – lights to see by and lights that allow you to be seen.

Be seen lights

Lights that allow you to be seen are emergency lights for when there is sufficient light to see where you are going, e.g. if there are street lights, it is early morning/dusk, there is mist/fog, but you need something to warn other road users that you are there. These lights will not provide enough light to see by.

Even if you are not intending to ride in the dark you should have a set of emergency, be seen, lights. Fog can descend without warning on high ground, even in the summer, and if you are riding on busy roads even a little spray from wet roads can render you almost invisible. There were two instances on my end to end where I needed my lights, one due to for fog in Scotland and one due to spray on the busiest section of road I used on the whole route.

There are a number of options be seen light options available, some so small and light you will not even notice that they are there. I use Knog frogs.

Top tips:

- Have emergency 'be seen' lights attached to your bike
- make sure your lights (inc emergency) are working before you set off on your trip. And take spare batteries/charger.
- Take a hand held torch or a head torch for reading road sign and route instructions. In an emergency the hand held torch could be zip tied to the handlebars if all other light options fail. I have a reasonably powerful led light no more than four inches long and extremely lightweight that cost £ 1.67 on ebay from Taiwan (inc batteries!) that I use for this purpose. I also use a head torch which has the advantage of pointing where you look but is a little awkward to wear with a helmet

Lights to see by

Lights to see by mean just that. There are various options at a wide range of prices providing various levels of just how much you can see! As you might expect, the more you pay the brighter the light and the lower the weight (in general).

Options:

Dynamo powered – lights wired to a dynamo (powered either through your wheel hub or a friction mechanism resting against your tyre wall). These provide the convenience of instant power at any time without having to carry batteries. You are the power source so there is a marginal amount of extra effort required (although with massive improvements in light technology, considerably less than a few years ago). The initial set up costs, especially for a hub powered system, may be higher than a battery light option.

Battery power – there are a wide range of battery powered lights that fall into two broad categories, rechargeable and non-rechargeable. The benefit of a rechargeable light is that you do not have to keep buying new batteries, which can prove to be expensive. The disadvantage is that if your light runs out of power before you reach your destination you are a bit stuck (unless you have a back-up light). I purchased a cat eye HL-EL610 rechargeable which provided good visibility at a reasonable cost. Also, on low power, it provided several hours of light. However, the first time I used it for more than a commute, on a proper night ride (on the night leg of a 600km in South West England) I ran into a problem. I had accidentally switched the light on during the day without realizing it and when I came to use it there was only about 15 minutes worth of power left! All I had left were my emergency Knog frogs, which would keep me visible but did not provide anything like enough illumination to cycle by. I was forced to tag onto another rider and travel at his higher pace. The result was, by the time we reached the sleep stop, several hours later, I was cooked and had to abandon. The lesson learnt was to carry a backup light! (Incidentally the person I cycled with had his dynamo fail on him but he had a backup light).

I now have a Hope 1 which provides excellent light output. Level one is easily sufficient for road use and it has three more brightness levels above this. I have comfortably cycled downhill at 25mph + without fear of hitting unseen obstructions on level four. It also has a 'be seen' flashing mode. This is not a rechargeable light but I use rechargeable cells. I purchased 2 sets of four 3200 mAh AA cells for about £10 on-line. They seem to provide about the same running time as Lithium cells. The main down side of this particular light is that once the battery power is used up it just cuts off. There is no dimming or warning, it just stops! This can be worrying if you are doing 30mph downhill at the time. I make sure to change to a fresh set of batteries long before the current set are to expire. Two sets will get me through a [summer] night.

Timing your trip will help on your lights strategy.

If you go at the end of June you will get about 16-17 hours of daylight to play with. If you try in December it will be more like 8 hours (or less in Scotland).

Do I need to take lights?

You should take emergency 'be seen' lights.

If you are planning long days in the saddle you should carry main lights in case you are delayed and have to finish in the dark.

If you are camping you could carry main lights that will double as camping lights.

If you are planning your trip in months of shorter daylight hours you should carry lights. The light levels at the beginning and end of these days can be particularly poor, especially if raining.

I took my Knog frogs <u>and</u> a Cateye TL-LD1100 main rear light to make sure I could be seen from behind.

Bags

Unless you are doing a supported ride you will need bags to put all your stuff in. Even if riding with support you will need to carry a minimum amount of kit like a spare inner tube, a multi tool, a rain cape and a mobile phone [to call the support vehicle when you need more stuff!].

Your bag(s) need to be big enough to carry all the stuff you want to put in them. But remember, you also have to be able to carry them, so concentrate your efforts on reducing the stuff rather than tracking down huge bags.

Get used to the weight and feel of your bags by doing a few cycles with them on the bike. If you commute to work start using them and add a bit of equipment every day or so to slowly get used to the weight and feel. A good training trick is to overload with weight so when you come to do the actual ride it is easier!

Bags come in many varieties (but check that you are able to fit them to your bike before purchasing any):

Saddle bags

As the name suggests, these attach to your saddle. They come in a range of sizes from tiny, just big enough for an inner tube and a pair of  tyre levers, to spacious 20+ litre capacity models.

I used a Carradice sqr tour bag (shown loaded for my 2014 LEJOG).

Technically it isn't a saddle bag because it attaches to a quick release mechanism that fastens to your seat post. This means you need to have sufficient seat post clear of the frame to clamp the release mechanism to, so check this before you buy.

The Carradice sqr tour bag has a capacity of 16 litres, most of which is contained in one large compartment, with two pockets on the outside which are handy for the things you might need in a hurry like a rain top, a gillet, inner tubes, tyre levers, multi tool and mobile phone. With the exception of the bits on the bike and on me, it swallowed my entire equipment list (see below), proved to be very water resistant and acted as a pretty efficient rear mudguard -it even has a plastic strip attached to the underside for the purpose. And whilst it looks like it might be unwieldy (see picture – Duncansby Head, Day Zero) it does not interfere with pedaling and (apart from the weight) doesn't affect handling, probably because it is behind the body and above the rear wheel. In fact it is so wieldy that it is normally attached to my bike for commuting in case I need to carry anything home.

Handlebar bags

These are very useful for carrying the things that you will need easily to hand, like food, rain cape etc, especially if you do not have nice big back pockets in your cycling jersey. It is also a good place to keep your camera for quick access for those impromptu shots. [But if you are going to do this try to get one with some padding inside (or add padding).]

Features to look out for are:

- map/route viewer
- quick release detach – if you keep all your valuables in it you can carry it into shops/cafes etc.
- Side pockets to hold small items
- Interior dividers
- Interior organisation for papers/maps/ routes/pens etc.

The downside of handlebar bags (and any bag on the front of the bike) is that steering is affected. It would be wise to do some training rides with the bag in place (and laden) to get used to the difference in handling.

Rack bags

You will need to have a luggage rack fitted to accommodate one of these bags. If you do not have frame fittings for a 'proper' rack you can get ones that attach to your seat post, providing you have a sufficient amount of seat post clear of the frame. [Although personally, if I was going to have to buy a seat post mounted rack and a rack bag I would go straight for a bag that attaches to the seat post like the Carradice sqr tour.]

Pannier bags

These are available for the front and the back of the bike. Most commonly used are rear panniers which attach to a luggage rack. In this case a seat post mounted rack will not suffice because it lacks the side framework to stop the bags interfering with the rear wheel.

If you're considering front panniers you are

getting into serious touring territory. You will need to have a front luggage rack fitted to your bike to accommodate the bags. If you are not camping then you are probably carrying too much!

Pannier bags can affect handling quite dramatically. To minimise this, ride with a pannier bag each side (front and/or rear) and try and distribute weight evenly between them. Stow heavier items at the bottom of the bags to keep the centre of gravity as low as possible.

Rucksacks

Whilst you can carry a lot in a rucksack they have little to recommend them for long distance cycling [personally speaking, for any kind of cycling]. All the weight is borne by your body causing aches and pains in neck, shoulder and back. As well as additional fatigue, your back sweats profusely and the weight is up high, making bike handling more difficult. The only benefits I can see are:

- the additional weight on your body might help you uphill, if you stand on the pedals.
- you can easily carry the bag into cafes and shops.

Stuff to put in bags

Your stuff to put in bags has to fit in your bags!

To re-iterate, it is better to reduce the quantity of stuff than to buy bigger/more bags to accommodate it. Is there anything you can do without? Really? Could you reduce things by using mutli purpose items, e.g. a phone that can take decent pictures/video, play music, send emails, act as a sat nav and you can read a book on?

On the next page is a list of all the things I took on my trip, which may help as a guide to the sorts of things you might need to take. Of course this is very much up to the individual and the type of trip you are planning. I was not camping and I also took the risk that I would not need things like spare spokes and tyres, for instance.

1. Me

2. Stuff to go on me:
   - Shorts
   - Tops
   - Leg warmers
   - Arm Warmers
   - Socks
   - Cycling shoes
   - Gloves
   - Helmet
   - 2-3 hour supply of food in pockets
   - Chest strap for heart rate monitor

3. Bike: Scott CR1 Team

4. Stuff to go on bike:
   - Bike computer
   - Sat Nav
   - Lights
   - Bottles
   - Pump
   - Route holder
   - Day's route
   - Bag

5. Stuff to go in bag:
   - Tyre levers
   - Multi tool
   - Inner tubes x2
   - Zip ties
   - Chain lube
   - Plastic bags
   - First aid kit
   - Antiseptic wipes
   - Butt cream
   - Toiletries
   - Mobile phone
   - Chargers (phone, sat nav, mp3)
   - MP3 player
   - Batteries
   - Lock
   - Book
   - Wallet
   - Route - paper
   - Camera
   - Sunglasses
   - Shorts (spare)
   - Top (spare)
   - socks (spare)
   - Wind stop/rain top
   - Gillet
   - Shoes – karate slippers
   - Long Sleeve top
   - Long Trousers – nylon hiking ¾ trousers
   - Spare food and energy drink powder for the day

Top tips:

- Select stuff to put in your bags not bags that will accommodate your stuff
- Pack things in clear plastic bags to keep them waterproof and to assist sorting through your kit

The only things I did not use on the trip were my pump, inner tubes, multi tool, first aid kit and mp3 player. Of those the only one I could have got away without carrying was the mp3 player. If desperate for space I could have also have managed without the spare cycling shorts and top but that would have meant starting in the early morning chill in slightly damp kit on a couple of days.

It is a good idea to pack your stuff in sealable, clear plastic bags. This will help to keep them watertight, preventing water leaking in and toiletries etc. leaking out. It also makes it much easier to sort through your kit.

Clothes

I don't know if anyone has completed a naked end-to-end on a bike. Someone has walked it naked (apart from boots, a hat and a rucksack). It took them seven months because they kept on getting arrested and spent two spells in jail en-route. A couple of lads cycled it in their underpants in 2009. In fact that's all they took – bikes and underpants, one pair each. They took no money so they had to blag everything else from food to accommodation to clean pants. I'm all for reducing the equipment list but that might be taking minimalism to an extreme!

So, for those of us that want to wear clothes on the ride:

What should I wear?

This is very much down to personal choice and

depends on what you are used to cycling in. Some people like to wear normal casual clothes that they feel comfortable in on or off the bike. Others like to wear technical cycling clothes designed specifically for the job. I once saw a rider in a time trial skin suit and a rider in corduroy trousers and an Argyll knitted tank top on the same sportive (the latter was passing the former up a very steep hill).

Not that I would recommend corduroy trousers and an Argyll knitted top for your trip. In fact I personally favour the technical cycling kit option for a number of reasons:

- It is shaped to fit the body most comfortably when in a cycling position.
- It does not [or at least should not] have any seams in positions that will rub.
- It is close fitting so cuts down wind resistance.
- The fabric is designed to draw (wick) sweat away from the skin to evaporate in the air.
- It is lightweight and packs down easily.
- Padded bottom area! [you have a very long way to go and you will be in the saddle a lot]
- Back pockets on cycling tops are ideal for carrying food and gels so that they are easily to hand without having to stop.
- Can be washed in the shower and dried out in an open window overnight.

The downside of cycling specific kit is that it is not ideal for wearing off the bike so you might have to carry some casual clothes if you intend to eat out or socialize in the evening. I took a pair of three quarter length lightweight hiking trousers and a long sleeved base layer, both of which were very light and could be packed down as small as possible. In the end the only time I wore them was on my journey to John O'Groats.

Shoes are another factor to consider. I have cycling shoes with cleats that attach to the pedals on my bike. This makes pedalling more efficient and requires less energy over a long distance. But it does make walking awkward when off the bike.

So I had to find a lightweight, easily packable pair of shoes for travel and evening wear, if required. I must admit that I struggled but in the end hit upon karate shoes. The pair I chose had a thin, hard, flat soles and the uppers were of silk and lay completely flat when not worn. They were a non-descript black and cost less than £5 online.

There are cleated cycling shoe/pedal systems with a recessed cleat so the shoe retains a flat sole, which are comfortable on and off the bike. These are very popular with regular tourers because they negate the need to carry additional 'off the bike' shoes. This requires the capital outlay for both new pedals and new shoes though and was out of my budget. But if you are intending to move to a cleated system or need to replace your shoes or pedals anyway it is a system worth looking at.

Regardless of whether you wear cycling specific or normal clothes you should aim to wear a number of thin layers that you can strip off or pile on depending upon the temperature and weather. One layer should be a rain jacket or cape because the chances of riding the entire length of Scotland and England (and maybe a bit of Wales) without being rained on are small. Very small.

The other necessity is padded shorts. If you prefer baggy shorts or trousers you can purchase padded short/trouser liners [no not a nappy]. If you have no padding take extra butt cream (see stuff to put in bags section).

This is a list of the clothing I took with me:

- Shorts (x2)
- Tops (x2)
- Leg warmers
- Arm Warmers
- Socks (x2 pairs)
- Wind stop/rain top
- Gillet
- Gloves
- Sunglasses
- Helmet
- Chest strap (for heart rate)
- Cycling shoes
- Other shoes – karate slippers
- Long Sleeve top – base layer
- Long Trousers – nylon hiking ¾ trousers

The shorts, tops and socks were duplicated in case I was unable to wash and dry them overnight. It meant I could wear a clean, dry set and strap the damp kit to the outside of my bags to dry [unless it was raining – obviously].

I set off each morning before 6:00am so even in early July it was chilly. So I would start each day with my shorts, top, arm and leg warmers, gillet and windstop/ rain top on. Then, as the day warmed up I would take off first the windstop/rain top, then the leg warmers and gillet and finally the arm warmers. If I was cycling late the reverse process happened in the evening.

You may notice as your tour progresses and you get tired that your body is less able to regulate your temperature. This means you will remain chilly for longer each day and strip off less and less. Certainly on my last day I cycled nearly all of it in my arm and leg warmers and a gillet despite it being a sunny (if windy) July day.

Remember that you have to carry your clothes so weight is an issue. Even if you are wearing most of it you still have to carry the weight. And packability is also an important factor. Some lightweight clothes (like fleeces) can still be very bulky and you need to be able to stow them all in your bags.

Final 'what should I take on my ride' check

Do this at least a week before your trip in case you need to amend your plans!

Lay out everything you intend to take on your trip and check it off your list. Then try and pack it into your selected bags. When packing, keep items that you are likely to need on the road accessible, in particular bike tools, spare tubes, pumps, sun cream etc. If after several attempts you cannot get it all in, you will either have to change bags or get rid of some stuff.

Once the bag(s) are packed to your liking, get someone to help you haul them to the bike and load it up. Hop aboard and ride a couple of miles down the road and back, preferably taking in at least one stiff hill. When you get back and have recovered sufficiently you can decide what you can do without!

Seriously, if you are not used to touring make sure you test ride the load before the start. Be careful because the bike will feel very different with a lot of extra weight, especially when setting off and around corners. Your braking will not be as sharp either!

Top Tip:

Wash your kit in the shower. Rub some soap or gel into the pad and other smelly bits and then dump it underfoot at the beginning of the shower. Tread it, like grapes, throughout the shower, trying not to trip or slip. Once you are clean give the kit a final rinse to make sure the soap is all out and then wring out as much water as possible. Once you have dried yourself lay your kit out flat on the towel and roll the whole thing up as tightly as possible. Repeat with a fresh, dry towel if you have one. Leave for a minute or two so that the towel can absorb any excess moisture. Unroll and hang your kit in an open window to finish drying overnight (or put on a radiator if there is one on).

Nutrition

I am not a nutritional expert but I have researched the subject in depth. What follows is a summary of much reading on the matter and hopefully distils the relevant points without getting too deep into the science.

I am going to say this at the very beginning and remind you again at the end of this section:

> Getting your nutrition right during training and on your trip will give you greater benefits than anything else you can do to prepare for the ride.

On a fundamental level this means making sure you consume the right amounts of food and drink at the right times. On a higher level it means eating and drinking the right things.

I have separated hydration out as a category in its own right because it is so important.

Your body needs fuel. More precisely it needs the energy contained in the fuel. The proper unit of measure for this energy is a kilojoule but a more commonly known unit is a calorie, expressed as cal or kcal. There are 4.2 kilojoules in a calorie.

The estimated average daily energy requirement for a normally active woman is 2,000 kcal or 2,500 for a man. These are figures for 'average' people and will vary depending on your size but can be used as good ball park figures.

Your body stores energy in the form of fat and as glycogen in the muscles and liver. The glycogen store, when fully topped up, equates to about 2,000 calories. The amount stored as fat varies from person to person but for most of us it is too much! The energy in fat is not as easily accessible as that stored as glycogen and to optimize energy release from your fat stores you need to be exercising at fairly low levels of intensity.

When exercising, your body requires more energy. It will obtain this energy from the most available source, which is food being processed by the stomach. If this is insufficient it will then deplete the glycogen supplies and then move on to either fat or protein (produced by breaking down muscle mass), depending on how much effort is being expended and how rapidly the energy is needed. Okay, it's not actually that simple but that linear view will be sufficient for our purposes: we're not top flight athletes.

The amount of additional energy you need will depend on the amount of effort you are putting in. On a fairly gentle recovery ride you might need an extra 3-400 calories per hour of riding. If you are powering along at maximum speed in hilly terrain the figure could be more like 800-1,000 per hour. Personally I don't get too scientific about it and work on an average of 600 calories per hour. So if I ride for 5 hours I need an extra 3,000 calories. This means that in total I should consume 5,500 in the day.

If I ate my normal 2,500 calories and let my body use up its entire 2,000 calories glycogen store (not wise – see box on Bonking on the Bike) I would still be 1,000 calories short. This could come from fat but if I am working hard it is much more likely to be extracted by breaking down the protein in my muscle. If I don't put any protein and energy back in, the net result is I am exhausted and my muscles are weaker than if I hadn't exercised in the first place.

So I need to put in lots of calories. In the above example more than twice as many as I would on a normal, non-cycling day. And ideally I should keep my glycogen supplies topped up as much as possible throughout the ride.

Where do the calories come from? Well, from what we eat. More specifically from:

Carbohydrates	100g	400 kcal
Protein	100g	400 kcal
Fat	100g	900 kcal
Alcohol	100g	700 kcal

Good new! That liquid lunch break at the pub is a brilliant way of topping up the glycogen supplies.

Sadly not.

Although alcohol contains a lot of energy per gram and is rapidly absorbed by the body, the available evidence suggests these Calories are not used significantly during exercise.

And unfortunately there are also negative effects:

- it is a diuretic and contributes to dehydration
- it slows down glycogen production and release from the liver so energy is slow to get to the muscles and the stores are not topped up quickly enough
- it can make you wobbly!

In fact studies have shown that cycling after taking alcohol requires more energy, produces a higher heart rate, and stimulates a higher cardiovascular demand. And you fall off a lot.

So what should I eat?

Having read all around the subject and found vastly conflicting views, it seems to me that the answer to good nutrition whilst training is not really any different to good nutrition when you are not training. You should eat a well-balanced diet combining carbohydrates (about 60%), protein (about 15%) and fat (about 25%) [and maybe a little alcohol]. You will need to eat more of it though to replenish the extra energy you are using.

Carbohydrates – 60%

Carbohydrates are the cyclist's main source of energy. They are basically either simple carbohydrates which the body can break down and utilise very quickly or complex ones that take a little longer. Put another way, some get used up very quickly and others are slow burners.

A useful tool is the Glycaemic Index. This gives a ranking of carbohydrates on a scale from 0 to 100 according to the extent to which they raise blood sugar levels after eating. The higher the GI a food has, the

Glycaemic Index (0-100)

Low GI Foods		Medium GI Food		High GI Foods	
Peanuts	14	Boiled potatoes	56	Mashed potato	70
Grapefruit	25	Sultanas	56	White bread	70
Red lentils	26	Pitta bread	57	Watermelon	72
Whole milk	27	Basmati Rice	58	Swede	72
Dried apricots	31	Honey	58	Bagel	72
Skimmed milk	32	Digestive biscuit	59	Branflakes	74
Low-fat fruit yoghurt	33	New potatoes	62	Cheerios	74
Wholemeal spaghetti	37	Coca cola	63	French fries	75
Apples	38	Raisins	64	Coco Pops	77
Noodles	40	Shortbread biscuit	64	Jelly beans	80
White spaghetti	41	Couscous	65	Rice cakes	82
All Bran	42	Rye bread	65	Rice Krispies	82
Peaches	42	Pineapple, fresh	66	Cornflakes	84
Porridge made with water	42	Croissant	67	Jacket potato	85
Baked beans in tomato sauce	48	Shredded wheat	67	Puffed wheat	89
Milk chocolate	49	Mars bar	68	Baguette	95
Wholemeal bread	53	Ryvita	69	Parsnips, boiled	97
Crisps	54	Weetabix	69	White rice, steamed	98
Banana	55	Wholemeal bread	69	Glucose	100

more rapidly digested and absorbed its energy is. I have included a table of some common food types but if you want to find the GI value of other foods visit www.glycemicindex.com/ which has an extensive database. Most people are surprised at the GI value of some foods the first time they come across them. For instance grapefruits, which are sweet and sugary are low GI and white rice, viewed by many as a bulk slow burner, is one of the highest GI foods going.

In general we should eat foods with low GI values to help maintain a steady blood sugar level. However, whilst on the bike we might need to use high GI food to provide a quick boost, especially if close to bonking. Personally, if I am going on a long ride I try to pack in some low GI foods before I start and then keep up a regular supply of medium/high GI foods interspersed with low GI foods whilst on the move. After the ride pack in more low GI foods to provide sustained energy for recovery.

Fat – 25%

Fat has long been labelled as an evil in dietary terms but it is an essential part of our nutritional needs. A lack of fat in the diet can adversely affect blood pressure and blood clotting, inhibit the body's ability to control inflammation and lead to low energy levels and poor recovery from exercise.

Fats come in three varieties:

- Saturated

  If any fats are 'evil' then these are they. These major contributors to heart disease have no known positive benefits for sporting performance or even health generally. Typically these fats are animal based, such as cheese and butter, and are widely used in processed foods. Of course most of us find them to be the tastiest fats as well.

- Monounsaturated

  Generally monounsaturated fats are widely believed to be the healthiest of all the fats. They are said to help reduce the bad form of cholesterol in the body and to increase the amount of good cholesterol. Sources of monounsaturated fats include nuts, seeds, avocados, olives and oils made from these products.

- Polyunsaturated

  These contain 'essential fatty acids' which the body cannot produce by itself and have to come from food. Whilst they can also reduce the harmful kind of cholesterol in the body they can also reduce the good cholesterol so need to be balanced with monounsaturated fats. Good sources of polyunsaturated fats are vegetable oils and oily fish.

Protein – 15%

The major consideration for a long distance cyclist is that protein's role in maintaining and replacing the tissues in your body. Your muscles, organs and many of your hormones are made up of protein, and it is also used in the manufacture of haemoglobin, the red blood cells that carry oxygen to your body. Protein is also used to manufacture antibodies that fight infection and disease and is integral to your body's blood clotting ability.

So you need protein to help your muscles repair after you have been punishing them all day, to maintain your red blood cell count so you don't need a transfusion every evening, to help fight off illness and to make sure you don't bleed to death from minor road rash.

Good sources of protein include:

- Meat – e.g. beef, poultry, pork and lamb
- Fish and shellfish
- Dairy products – e.g. cheese, yogurt and milk
- Eggs
- Beans, peas, oats and legumes
- Tofu and soy products
- Nuts and seeds

For post ride recovery try a yoghurt after a short ride or a milkshake after a longer effort. It can be worth trying a carbohydrate and protein recovery drink after an all-day effort to maximise recovery before the next day. On my JOGLE I tried to make sure I drank a whey protein drink as soon after the end of each day's ride as possible.

There is also evidence to suggest that protein can help the body in the processing of glycogen and that consuming protein and carbohydrate in a ratio of 1:4 optimises the absorption rate. You can buy sports drinks made up in this proportion. Personally I find them heavy on my stomach but replicated the effect on my JOGLE by eating half a protein bar about every couple of hours.

Micro Nutrients and Vitamins

Whilst carbohydrates, proteins and fats provide the body with fuel (as well as other things) it also needs a variety of other things in order to function properly. These are broadly termed micronutrients and include things like vitamins, minerals and enzymes. The body needs these to maintain the body's immune and hormone system (you'll need some adrenalin to get you up those hills), to repair body tissues and to control nerve and muscle function and fluid levels.

Mystery Superfood

And the superfood is – milk! No really. Not only is it an excellent source of protein, it contains good levels of carbohydrate, packs a range of vitamins and minerals and hydrates you as well. When you're training hard, drink one to two pints a day. This sounds a lot, but you'll feel the difference when you recover quicker and whizz through that training.

The best way to make sure you are getting the micro nutrients you need is to eat your 'five a day' fruit and vegetable portions. Although, when you are training hard and using twice as much energy as usual, you will also need to up your micro nutrients. So you may have to eat ten a day. [Please note that whilst wine is made from grapes it does not count as one of your five a day. Nor does cider. Or any other alcoholic beverage.]

You should strive to maintain the balance of 60/15/25 (or so) at each meal to provide the body with a steady stream of all the things it needs. Of course this is not always particularly easy when you are on the road for possibly 12 hours or more a day. Even if you stop for proper meals you will still need to maintain a steady supply between stops if you do not want to suffer from peaks and troughs in performance. Which is why most professional endurance cyclists use a predominantly sports drink, energy bar and energy gel diet when in competition.

How much do I need to eat?

Finally I would like to point out is just how much you will have to eat on your ride. Actually that's not true, I don't know how long you are intending to cycle every day or how fast you intend to ride or how hilly your route is or how big you are etc.. The point is it may be more than you think.

To illustrate, this is how I estimated my calorie intake. I worked on an average calories consumption of 600 kcal per hour (I was between 70 and 75 kg during my ride). Each day I was intending to travel approximately 150 miles spending about 12 hours in the saddle. So 12 x 600 = 7,200 kcal. Say **8,000 kcal** per day because I would be burning some energy in the other 12 hours of the day.

Food	Serving	Kcal
Potato Baked, Flesh & Skin	1 Med/180g	245
Banana Fresh	1 Med/150g	143
Apricots, Dried	1 Serving/50g	83
Pear	1 Med/170g	68
Orange	1 Med/160g	59
Apple	1 Med/112g	53
Pasta – white	100g (uncooked)	357
Rice – long grain	100g (uncooked)	358
Bread – multi grain	100g	250
Chicken - roasted	100g	128
Pork sausage	One link	48
Heinz Baked Beans	can 540g	396

To put this in context the consumption of an average man should be about 2,500 kcal per day or 2,000 for a lady.

You can see from the table of calories contained in some basic food item that to consume 8,000 kcal I would have to eat 32 baked potatoes or 56 bananas or 20 large cans of beans or 166 pork sausages (!) each day to replenish my energy supplies.

Unless I wanted to spend a huge amount of time

off the bike in café's etc. I would have to find a way to eat the bulk of this on the move. I tried stuffing my pockets with 32 baked potatoes but they didn't fit [not really] and I would look ridiculous with a string of 166 sausages looped round and round my shoulders [that is true] so I had to find something which packed the calories into a smaller package. For me it was energy bars, cereal bars, protein bars and energy drinks supplemented with bacon sandwiches, pasties, pot noodles and multi vitamins. Not to everyone's taste but it worked for me!

Here is a list of what I worked out I would need to eat each day:

	Quantity	Calories
Energy bars	6	1284
Protein bars	4	940
Energy Gels	3	460
Energy gels with Caffeine	3	460
Recovery Drink	1 litre	1373
Energy Drink	6 litres	1555
Cereal Bars	6	900
Pot Noodle	1	250
Oat Biscuits	100g	430
Bacon Sandwich		500
Total		8152

Please note that this is not the world's best diet! It is lacking in many ways but was based on the fact that I only needed to maintain it for six days. In those six days my main concerns were energy and muscle recovery. My diet during my training period was based on the balanced diet discussed above [vaguely].

Of course everyone likes different things to eat and drink, some are restricted in diet medically or through belief and we all have different approaches as to how we want to eat whilst on a ride. Many people like to make regular stops to eat and drink and it becomes an integral part of the ride, a chance to have a break from pedalling and to socialise for a while (especially if riding solo). Others, like me, pack our pockets and chaff at every stop or slight detour from our route to have to deal with the tedious task of loading up with food and liquid again.

Whatever your preferences you will need to think about the logistics of nutrition. In some areas there can be long stretches between places to eat. And if you are riding a route using major roads these bypass most towns and you can ride for hours without passing any shops or even services on the road.

So you have to balance how much you can carry and how much you can buy en-route each day. My strategy had one major flaw – where could I buy sports energy bars, drinks and protein supplements en-route every day? I certainly couldn't carry them all with me and even if I could I'd have to get them to John O'Groats and the start line. My solution was to post each day's supplies to myself. I had pre-booked B&Bs so arranged for the owners to receive a 'red cross' parcel with all my supplies of the next day at each destination. As long as the parcels arrived I would be ok. It also gave me an added incentive to complete my mileage every day. [As it happened I found it very difficult to eat everything so ended up carrying an increasing weight of surplus food because I was too tight to throw it away. I got really hungry on day four though and ate most of it!]

Hydration

When out on your bike have you noticed any of

the following symptoms towards the end of a ride?:

- increased heart rate
- increased breathing rate
- increased body temperature
- fatigue
- muscle cramps
- headache
- nausea

I would be most surprised if you haven't. Most of us put this little list of common cycling ailments down simply to not being as fit as we should be. Whilst this is probably true and will not help the situation, it is much more likely that the main cause of all or any of these symptoms is dehydration.

Your body is over 70% water. So you can imagine that it is quite important stuff. Unfortunately the body uses it up and leaks it out so we have to drink to top our supplies up.

There is a lot of scientific research about what happens when we become dehydrated; which are the first parts of the body to dry up and die etc.. All pretty gruesome reading. But, without getting into the whys and wherefores, the consequences of not keeping your water tanks full (becoming dehydrated) are generally agreed as the list above. The amount you have to become dehydrated to experience these symptoms varies from research to research but you should start to suffer from them if you are 3-5% dehydrated. This means your water tanks are 3-5% empty.

However, research has also shown that the body's ability to produce energy can be significantly affected by even a small drop in hydration and that this increases with each further percentage drop. When you bear in mind other research that suggests we generally operate at 1% dehydrated this means that normally we are under performing from the moment we get on our bikes. Then as the ride progresses, if we put in less liquid than we leak out, our ability to produce energy gets worse and our performance suffers. If we let our water tanks deplete to the 3-5% level we being to suffer the more severe symptoms listed above.

If you become 10% dehydrated you can expect:

- muscle spasms
- vomiting
- racing pulse
- shrivelled skin
- dim vision
- confusion
- painful urination
- difficult breathing
- seizures
- unconsciousness
- chest and abdominal pain

Of course if you are grinding up a 20% climb you might well have a racing pulse and difficulty breathing and arguably you must have been pretty confused to go that way in the first place. And the two bottles of red wine (lots of antioxidants) you got through last night might account for the shrivelled skin, dim vision and vomiting. So just because you have some of these symptoms doesn't necessarily mean you need hospitalization. Just be aware. Especially if you consider that if you become more than 10% dehydrated you might die.

Now, that is all very good, but you do not actually have water tanks with handy gauges to tell you how full of water you are, so how can you tell? The most obvious indicator the body has for dehydration is thirst. Unfortunately the consensus of scientific opinion seems to be that you are already 2-3% dehydrated before you feel thirsty. So if you wait until you are thirsty you are already substantially underperforming and getting close to the first list of symptoms.

Top tips:

- Eat little and often. Set a timer to remind you to eat if necessary. Eat even if you are not hungry – you have a lot of calories to consume!
- Listen to your body. If it starts craving bacon its probably after protein, if its chocolate you need carb energy fast. Get a sugary fix AND eat some slower burners otherwise you will 'crash' again quickly.
- Down protein after your ride each day to improve your recovery. Try to do it as soon after the end of the ride as possible. There is an optimum window of between 10-20 minutes after the ride when the body can make best use of the protein to repair muscles and aid recovery.
- On long rides consume carbs and protein in a 4:1 ration. This will aid energy levels and boost recovery.
- Caffeine can help your concentration levels towards the end of a long ride but don't overdo it. Carry emergency caffeine gels.
- Things can taste sweeter towards the end of a long ride so if you are using energy drinks dilute them a little more as the day progresses.

Another indicator is the colour of your wee. When fully hydrated it should be the colour of pale straw (nice subjective term for you to argue over with your riding companions – "Does this look like pale straw to you?"). The point is, your body starts to regulate water when the level in the tanks starts to go down. Less is leaked out in your urine so it becomes darker in colour. If you notice it becoming darker during a ride you need to start drinking more. Of course it is not always that easy. On long rides I ride with one bottle of energy drink and one of water with an isotonic tablet in it that contains various vitamins and minerals. The side effect of the tablet is that my wee becomes bright, luminous yellow, which is great fun for weeing in the dark but not so good for judging my hydration levels.

So, it is always best to know your own body and to have some idea of how dehydrated you are getting whilst riding over various distances. I know I am normally good at keeping topped up over shorter rides but I lose discipline on longer ones. To judge your hydration levels weigh yourself before and immediately after a ride. Any weight you have lost in kilos is equivalent to fluid loss in litres (roughly 1lb loss = 1 pint). So if you have lost 2 kg you have used up 2 litres from your tanks. This needs to be replaced at 1½ x the fluid loss so you will need to drink 3 litres of water to fill your tanks. And also means you should have drunk this much more on your ride.

Dehydration

List One – 3-5%

- increased heart rate
- increased breathing rate
- increased body temperature
- fatigue
- muscle cramps
- headache
- nausea

List Two – 10%

- muscle spasms
- racing pulse
- shriveled skin
- dim vision
- painful urination
- confusion
- difficult breathing
- seizures
- chest and abdominal pain
- unconsciousness

List Three - >10%

- complete inability to function due to death

If you have gained weight during your ride you should consider spending less time on the pub break next time.

Also take into consideration the temperature and riding conditions. You will need to drink much more in hot sunny conditions than in cold wet ones. And a flat route will probably result in less liquids leaking out of you than a hilly one.

Even so, most of your fluid loss will be due to sweat.

This means that your body will be losing vital salts as well. Make sure that these are replaced. The easiest way to do this is with isotonic drinks and gels or with isotonic tablets added to your water bottles.

So the answer is to know your body and drink, preferably little and often. And if you get thirsty you have not drunk enough and you need to immediately increase your intake.

The little and often is important on longer rides and tours. Ideally you should eat and drink a little every 20 minutes or so to maintain a steady

Sports drink concentration

- **Isotonic** (5-8% sugar) sports drinks contain similar concentrations of salt and sugar as in the human body. Ideal for consumption during normal riding conditions.

- **Hypotonic** (<5% sugar) sports drinks contain a lower concentration of salt and sugar than the human body. These are easily absorbed by the body and most useful in hot conditions when hydration is a greater issue than calorie intake or after exercise if you finish in a dehydrated state.

- **Hypertonic** (>10% sugar) sports drinks contain a higher concentration of salt and sugar than the human body. These are difficult to absorb and can be bad for hydration. If you are well hydrated after a ride they can be used to replenish energy stores.

supply of water and energy to the body. In most of my training rides I am fairly undisciplined and often forget to do this. Or if I do remember it tends to be at an inconvenient time like zooming down a twisty descent and by the time I've reached the bottom I've forgotten again. When I do finally remember at a convenient place I then cram in food and water until I feel overly full and uncomfortable and don't want to do either again for a while, so forget again. The result is that I get patches where I feel really good and others were I feel really bad, corresponding to the levels of water and energy from food in my system.

On my JOGLE I was much more concentrated. I was painfully aware that my target of 150 miles as day was really going to stretch me. In my training I had only once managed to do two consecutive days of 100 miles plus and that had ended in me abandoning the ride suffering like a dog (strange term – my dogs live a life of luxury) and vomiting on the side of the road (dogs do do that – I didn't proceed to eat mine back down though). My later research on hydration showed I was suffering from severe dehydration, well beyond list one and approaching list two.

I knew that if I didn't put in enough water and food I would not only suffer later in the day I would suffer the next day as well. So I set a timer to beep every half hour to remind me to eat and drink. On the whole it worked pretty well. My energy levels remained fairly constant throughout the day. Admittedly the energy levels were less each day but that was just fatigue. On any given day I found my speed and power output did not tail off too much towards the end of the day. Although I was very thankful to stop.

Final Word on Nutrition

I know I have whittered on about nutrition but that is because it is so important, especially on a tour of several days or more. My personal opinion is that getting your eating and drinking right will have a greater impact on how you feel and perform on your end-to-end than getting your training right will.

Of course eating and drinking right doesn't mean

you don't have to do the training. Sorry. But if you can get the eating and drinking right <u>during</u> your training as well, you will get much more out of it. Firstly it won't be as painful, secondly you will recover from each training ride more rapidly and thirdly, your fitness will improve more quickly.

Finally I would point out that training when dehydrated and with low energy levels can be a wasted effort or even detrimental. I know riders who pride themselves on being able to complete a 100 mile ride on one 500ml water bottle and a lick of a flapjack wrapper. I can't help thinking how much better they would feel and how much fitter they would become if they weren't so hard.

Budget

If you are anything like me, thoughts about the cost of preparing for and undertaking your end to end get a low billing [excuse the pun]. Right up until the time it comes to start paying for things! Also, if you are like me, you will not have a pile of cash hanging around to deal with all the associated costs. Further, if you are like me, you won't have appreciated how much it is going to cost [coz riding a bike is free - right!?!]

This is where the money will go (I have included an estimate of my costs but these costs are extremely variable):

- Travel to the start/from the finish [Plane to start - £100. Petrol for car to airport and from finish £50].
- Accommodation en-route [Six nights B&B £180].
- Food/energy bars/drinks etc. during ride [£200]
- Equipment – do you need stuff to put on your bike, e.g., lights and bags, stuff to put in bags? [Carradice sqr tour bag £48, Gamin 705 Sat Nav £250]
- New bike(?) – whether you need to persuade yourself or your spouse, this is a good excuse for a new bike, especially if you're riding for charity (although if it's

your spouse that needs persuading it may be prudent to accidentally spill ink over this section of the book to cover the trail) [Scott CR1 team 2008 £999 – I needed a new bike anyway...honest...no really, I did...and it was for charity after all...]

- Training - training costs are for food (energy bars, drinks etc..) on training rides and for the bike parts you might wear out. If you are not used to regularly putting in lots of miles you will be surprised how quickly you start to go through tyres (approx. every 2,000 miles), brake blocks (500 miles – 2,000 miles depending on weather conditions and terrain, chains (1-2,000 miles), cassettes (3-5,000 miles) and cables for brakes and gears. The harsher the weather the faster things will wear out. And you should try and train in all weather conditions. [I did 5,000 miles of training and spent about £200 on parts and £200 on energy bars, drinks etc. I also spent a considerable sum on café meals but haven't factored them in because they were normal meals that would have been eaten whether I was cycling or not (although probably not in a café)].

- Pre-ride service - you should also budget for a full service at your local bike shop to make sure your chosen stead is up to the job. However, try not to be persuaded that what you really need is a nice new team issue racing bike (unless you want to be persuaded of course [or need the help of professional advice to persuade other (dis)interested parties]). [£80 including boxing and shipping bike to another bike shop in Wick – see section on getting to start.]

The total cost for me was £2407 but this did include a new bike and sat nav @ £1249.

So, having discovered that cycling is not 'free' I will work out how much my next adventure is going to cost in the early planning stages and save up for it in advance.

Middle

Right. So you've worked out how you are going to get to the start and from the finish, you've selected a bike, decided what you're going to wear and what to take with you and you've thought about what you're going to need to eat and drink during training and on the ride. All you need to do now is plan in some training and create a route.

Training

How much training do I need to do and when should I do it?

How much training will depend on your current fitness level and what the objectives of your ride are. If you are a regular cyclist and you intend to take a leisurely three week tour your training requirements will be somewhat less than someone who hasn't been on a bike since they were a kid, doesn't do much exercise to be honest and wants to complete a charity end-to-end in a week.

As to when – preferably before the ride!

In truth, if you are an active cyclist and you are taking a couple of weeks for the trip you might get away without any training at all, providing you are prepared to suffer a bit on the way. By active I mean that you are used to riding distances of 70 miles plus and cycle at least an average of 50 miles a week, every week.

If you are intending to take less time you will need to do some training, unless you are already pretty fit.

What sort of training should I do?

You can use your training to improve your speed

and/or your endurance. Probably the most pertinent will be endurance but you may wish to improve your speed if you are hoping to cover a lot of miles a day and want as long as possible to recover before you start again the next day.

The basic principle of any training is to stress the body so that it adapts to the new pressures being put on it. There are two main factors here, firstly you have to push the body harder than you normally do in order to achieve any gains and secondly you need to give the body time to recover and rebuild itself after each stress session. If you do not do both of these things you will not get full value out of your training.

In terms of improving your endurance you will need to concentrate on increasing the duration and frequency of your rides at a given level of effort. To up your speed you will need to increase the intensity of your riding using intervals to push your body's capacity to process oxygen and nutrients more rapidly.

Your main concentration will be endurance training. We are not pros so I'm am not going to get technical about heart rates and power outputs and red blood cell concentrations and lactate levels and so on. There is great benefit to be had from these things but not for the purpose of touring from one end of the country to the other (unless you are going for a record - but then you should know what you are doing in terms of training already [and won't be reading this book!]. I rode with a heart rate monitor on the ride (and during training), mainly to make sure I didn't over cook it and suffer later on.

Fundamentally, to increase endurance you have to ride further than you normally do. Very simple (but not necessarily easy). The secret is to build up by no more than 10-15% per week. That way your body can cope with the adaptation without becoming exhausted.

Comfortably

By 'comfortably' I mean you are not exhausted and haven't struggled to turn the pedals over for the last few miles. I do not mean you get off the bike feeling fresh and bright. A good indication would be to imagine how you would react if someone asked you to cycle another 10 miles: if the colour red or any images involving guns, knives, red hot pokers or similar leap to mind then it probably wasn't comfortable.

As an example, let's say you had a target ride of 100 mile taking place on 1st June. Back track through the calendar 8 weeks to the beginning of April. This is where training, ideally, should begin. Your training goal will be to be able to comfortably (see box) ride 75% of the target distance (75 miles) as one long ride by the time of the event. If at the beginning you can comfortably ride 35 miles then your first week target would be 40 mile. Then ramp up by about 5 mile a week until by the time of the event you are covering a distance of 75 miles.

These training distances are for one long ride a week. However, to increase your fitness you really need to be riding twice this distance in total every week. And you should ride at least four times a week. So, for example, in the final week of training you might be looking to ride one 75 miler and three 25 milers.

A simple chart would look like this:

	Base	1	2	3	4	5	6	7	8	Event
Single Ride	35	40	45	50	55	60	65	70	75	100
Other rides		40	45	50	55	60	65	70	75	

Perhaps the best way to get the other rides in is to bike to work if you are able. This is a great way of stealing training time and you can use the getting home sessions, when it doesn't matter if you get too hot and sweaty, to do some interval work to improve your speed and cardiac response if you need to.

If you have more than 6-8 week before an event you can use the extra time to build your base fitness up so that you are able to easily cover half the event distance by the time you come to the eight week intensive period.

Of course the end to end is not a one off event. You will be getting up day after day to repeat your efforts and therefore you will need to put in more training than just to cover 75% of your targeted daily distance. If you are intending to ride 100 miles a day you should train up to that distance and feel comfortable at the end of it. You should also make sure you have completed at least 75% of your daily distance on two or three consecutive days without feeling exhausted.

Because you will be doing some fairly intensive training you must build in rest periods every 3-4 weeks. This will allow your body to recover and grow stronger. This doesn't mean you get to have a week off. You have to continue to cycle but reduce the distance to about half of what you were doing (or should have been doing) in the preceding week.

When training you should try to replicate the conditions you will face on your end to end as much as possible. This means cycling on the types of roads you are planning to use, riding in all weather, covering the same sort of terrain, using the same sort of rest periods and eating the same kinds of foods.

The nutrition element is very important. For instance, I planned to live mainly on energy bars and gels. It would have been a disaster to get to the ride and find I couldn't stomach them as a main food source for several days. So, as well as using them on most of my training rides I carried them as my sole energy source on a 600km Audax ride through Devon, Cornwall and Somerset to make sure I could survive on them. As it happened I couldn't. I reached the point of throwing up at the side of the road on the second day and had to abandon. True, this was largely due to sun stroke from the day before but that in turn was caused by my not drinking either enough or the right stuff. It taught me to ride with one bottle of energy drink and a second of just water with an effervescent mineral, vitamin and electrolyte tablet dissolved in it.

Aside from getting you fit, training is also important in ironing out any problems you might encounter that could put an end to your ride. If you are not used to riding for long periods you might start to notice sores and pains that you have not encountered before. These might be caused by your riding position or technique and training is a good opportunity to make small adjustments to try and correct any issues. Personally I started to develop lower back pain and sciatica during training. With a bit of experimentation I discovered it was caused by driving too hard up very steep hills whilst sat in the saddle. Or probably, more correctly, not having good technique when cycling up hill and hence stressing the muscles in the lower back causing pain and inflammation, which led to the sciatica. Unfortunately many of the Audax routes I was using for training seemed to relish in 20% plus hills so I had to learn to stand in the saddle, which I always find tiring over any distance.

Of course you will almost inevitably suffer to some degree with saddle sores, although getting used to being in the saddle for extended periods in training will help to toughen up 'the area'. Prevention is better than cure and I would recommend clean shorts every day, starting the day with a good spread of butt cream of your choice (my personal recommendation is Sudocrem – slightly antiseptic, cheap and gentle enough for my baby's bottom, so good enough for me), and antiseptic wipes for clean-up and re-application half way through the day.

Training plan example

As an example, I have set out below how I planned my training.

I had devised a main road route and needed to ride about 150 miles a day to complete the tour in six days. I started training about 6 months before the event so I had lots of time to build up my base miles.

During training I commuted to work on my bike which amounted to about 110 miles a week. This was a great base to be starting from because it meant my body was used to riding several days in a row. All I had to do was get it to a state where it could do about 7 times the distance each day.

My plan was to build up to being comfortably able to cover a 100 mile distance by the time I got to the intensive training period, 8 weeks before the ride. I planned one long ride each weekend starting at about 50 miles and slowly building up to the 100 miles. From there I would ramp up until I could complete a 150 mile ride two days consecutively, with a recovery week 5 weeks before the event.

I would also extend my commutes to work slightly each week to increase my base miles and get my body used to cycling longer on a daily basis.

	Base	1	2	3	4	5	6	7	8	Event
Single Ride	100	110	120	130 +70	60	130	140 +75	150 x2	150	6x150
Other rides	110	110	130	150	110	130	150	170	64	

The final 150 mile ride was planned for the weekend before the event. In the week leading up to the event I commuted to work on the Monday as a recovery ride from the 150, nothing on the Tuesday, a recovery commute on Wednesday, nothing on Thursday and then a recovery 20 mile ride on the Friday from Wick to John O'Groats. All with the aim of being fresh and perky, raring to go at 6 O'clock Saturday morning.

Good plan.

What really happened was somewhat different. I never did increase my commuting mileage because, let's face it, getting to work is *always* a mad panic. In fact, with one thing and another, I didn't manage to commute everyday of every week. And making up a couple of lost commutes at the weekend as well as a long ride just doesn't happen. And of course not all the long rides happened. And when they did they were normally a bit longer than anticipated because I was trying to catch up lost rides (and if you're going to ride 85 miles you might as well make it a 100).

So I didn't put in all the miles I had planned and my lovely tapered profile looked more like a saw blade with broken teeth. But I did intensify my training in the last couple of months, riding at least one 100 mile plus ride each weekend.

What I didn't do was cycle on the types of road I would be using on the ride. This was largely because there aren't a lot of main roads [at least what the rest of the country calls main roads] near my home. And also the terrain I trained on was somewhat different to most of my route. Having done nearly all of my cycling in Devon and Cornwall I was most surprised (pleasantly) to find that most of my route was relatively flat. This worked well for me because, whilst I hadn't completed all the miles I had planned in training, the miles I had put in were much harder than the miles I would have to cover on my ride. A 150 mile ride through twisty, gravely lanes, constantly up and down 10% + hills with little or no flat in between is more draining than 150 miles of gently undulating main road (at least physically).

Not training on the same terrain worked out well

of me because I went from hard to easy (relatively speaking). If you come from a flat area and are planning a sight seeing tour through Cornwall, Devon, the Cotwolds, the Lakes and the smaller roads of Scotland then you need to find some hills to train in. Or failing that, ride with your back brake half on.

No matter what you have planned it is inevitable that life will get in the way. Ultimately you will have to do what you can and then try and polish your fitness on the ride.

As a final word on training, make sure you agree your training plan with your partner, if you have one. Remember that they will probably be taking on a lot of extra household burdens, plus possibly ferrying you around to events. That's not to mention having to listen to your constant barrage of moans and groans (lows) and excited speculations and hypothesizing about the ride itself (highs).

If you are lucky enough to have a partner by the end of the venture a little thanks would not go amiss.

Route creation

In principle this is easy. You have a defined start and finish and it is basically up or down, depending on where you start. Of course the reality is not so simple. There are many factors to take into account:

- How long are you planning for the tour? Do you have time to wander or will you have to go in as straight a line as possible?
- What sort of roads do you like to cycle on – flat, hilly, narrow, wide, quiet or busy (Busy roads do have some advantages: drag from lorries and juggernauts, they tend to be less hilly, average speeds are higher and there are actually less hazards on the main roads - but

the consequences of an incident are much worse, so you're less likely to have an accident or a spill but if you do you'll probably be dead.)

- Do you want to go as direct as possible or do you want to make sure you cover at least a 1000 miles as an extra challenge?
- Why are you doing the trip – sightseeing or just to get there?
- Are there specific places you would like to see?, e.g. St Ives, Dartmoor, Bath, Chester, Lake District, Gretna Green, Loch Ness, Cairngorms.
- Do you want an extra challenge? For instance you might want to incorporate some extra UK mainland 'extremes' with little extra mileage, e.g. most southerly point (Lizard Point) – most north easterly point (Duncansby Head – *not John O'Groats!*) – most northerly point (Dunnet Head).
- What sort of accommodation are you going to use? Is it conveniently on your proposed route?

In most parts of the country there are many road options to get from A to B, so picking the right one is entirely dependent on your own personal preferences. That is why I am not proposing that you use the route I rode. For a start it would lead you direct to the door of each B&B I used and I wouldn't necessarily endorse all of them! And anyway, they may no longer be trading as B&Bs.

What you need is a methodology to create your own route, based upon your own requirements. I am sure that many of you have tried and tested route creation techniques but others may feel, like I did, a little daunted at tackling a 900 mile route.

I started with a road atlas. I used the primary road map at the front to fix the basic route with the distance table providing the ballpark stopping points, based upon how far I intended to ride each day – 150 miles. This process pegged key points somewhere around John O'Groats, Fort Augustus (on Loch Ness), Glasgow, Windermere (Lake District), Shrewsbury, Taunton and Land's End.

Having broken the 900 miles down into six daily chunks I then turned to the more detailed pages to try and find the most favourable roads for each day. With my requirements of speed and distance in mind I looked at the primary routes first. Where possible I selected old primary roads that often run alongside newer ones. They are usually in good condition but much quieter than the new road or motorway that has taken their place. Where the road looked good I marked it in with pen. Where I wasn't sure I left blanks.

Having completed this process I had a road atlas with a route marked most of the way through the country but with big gaps around Glasgow and right through the midlands. Quite frankly the midlands had me quite scared. The road atlas was just a big spaghetti splat of twisting red, blue and green lines. I got headaches trying to follow roads from one page to the next. Having no local knowledge of the area it looked like a nightmare of urban sprawl. And the same was true of Glasgow but to a lesser extent, being a smaller area.

In the end I bit the bullet and penned in my line on the road atlas through the midlands but was still left with my Glasgow gap. So I turned to the internet and searched on www.google.co.uk [other search engines are available] for bike routes through Glasgow. I quickly found many possibilities and ultimately decided on a route that got me off the A82 at the first opportunity, to cross the Erskine Bridge. This avoided the bulk of Glasgow completely but directed me more westerly than I had originally intended. However, although it added a few extra miles to the route, ultimately it meant quieter but still primary route roads.

So, I now had my rough route marked in pen on my atlas.

My next step was to find B&B accommodation at roughly 150 mile steps. With my Glasgow bypass this would now be roughly Fort Augustus, Kilmarnock, Windermere, Shrewsbury and Taunton. I returned to Google and searched for 'B&B Fort Augustus' and was presented with a list of options. I browsed each site to decide which was the most suited to my needs (close to route/en-suite if possible/cheap) and made contact with my preferred option asking:

a) if they had single availability on my chosen date.
b) if they had anywhere I could store my bike.
c) if they would be willing to accept delivery of a parcel on my behalf a couple of days before my arrival.
d) whether arriving late in the day would be a problem.
e) what the cost was.

I then booked the best option and printed out a directions map from the website to show the B&B's location compared to my main road route.

This process was then repeated for the other stopping areas. My only sticking points in the process were in the Lake District and around Taunton. In the former I ended up in Kendal rather than Windermere (because it was considerably cheaper) and in the latter I found few options near the route and had to detour down some twisty lanes for a few miles (as it turned out a detour well worth taking for the accommodation – see day 5 in the section describing my route).

Fortunately, probably because I was booking a few months in advance, I managed to get into my first choice accommodation at each stopping point.

I marked the B&Bs on my atlas and re-jigged the

route accordingly. So now I had my entire route penned in on the atlas (a little messy in areas). However, I had decided that I didn't want to carry any paper maps with me (no room in my bag – full of other stuff!) so what I really wanted was a written route sheet telling me which way to turn at each junction and the distances between instructions. Having taken out a small mortgage to buy a sat nav I thought it would be a good idea to have the route on there as well. The sat nav also had a map of the whole UK on it as back-up, providing the battery didn't give up at the critical moment.

Back on the internet I Googled 'bike route creation'. At the time there were only a couple of options available and I chose www.bikely.com. Following the instructions I created a separate route for each stage and then laboriously followed the route through on screen, writing down instructions of what to do at each junction and the distance to that point. These were later typed up to create my route sheet.

Since then I have discovered a much better way to create directions and gpx files by using Google Maps (see below).

Of course what you actually take with you in terms of directions and maps is a matter of personal preference. You could just set off with a list of town names you are going to pass through or near and navigate by road signs. Or you might want to have written directions and detailed maps of the whole route.

Whilst I did without maps I did have a very detailed route sheet. And when I did lose my way I used my portable navigation device to put me back on track. [Not my sat nav, which I hadn't mastered when I started the ride. I used my mobile to call my wife who told me where to go. Luckily she got out the road atlas and gave me directions as well.]

How to create a route using Google Maps

The first step is to open your web browser and search for 'google my maps' (see Route Creation One).

Route Creation One

On the next screen click 'Create a New Map' (see Route Creation Two).

If you are not already logged into a google account you will be prompted to log in or create an account. If you need to create an account follow the instructions on screen and then, if necessary, start this process from the top.

On the next screen, first click on the directions icon near the top, middle of the map. This will open a box on the left where directions can be inserted. Type in your start point in the 'A' box and your destination in the 'B' box (see Route Creation Three where the start location is slightly obscured by the pop up box). The more precise you can be the less fiddling you will

Route Creation Two

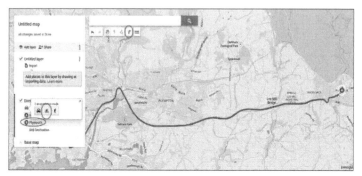

Route Creation Three

have later [you can even put in grid references]. A driving route should appear on the map.

Now click on the word 'driving' next to the car symbol and click the bicycle icon on the pop up. The map should now show cycle routes in addition to roads and it is likely that the route will adjust to select Google's suggested cycle route. This is shown in Route Creation Four (ignore the branch off to 'C' for the moment).

You can add more destination points by clicking on 'Add destination'. You can then rearrange the order of the destinations by dragging and dropping the letters by the typed destinations. Route Creation Four shows the screen just before releasing the move of the added destination 'Sparkwell' to be between Ivybridge and Plymouth. The route line is still showing

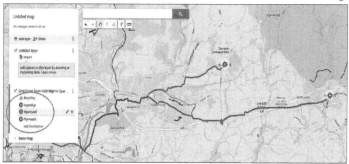

Route Creation Four

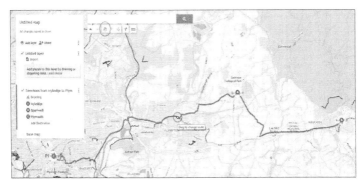

Route Creation Five

the route as Ivybridge to Plymouth to Sparkwell.

Route Creation Five shows the map once the 'Sparkwell' destination has been moved.

You may now wish to fine tune your route. The first thing to do is check that the start and finish locations are correct. To do this point your mouse cursor just below the 'A' and double left click. This should zoom you in on the map. You may need to repeat this process a couple of times to get sufficient detail. Alternatively you can use the roller on your mouse to zoom in and out if you have one.

If the start position is not quite in the right place then drag and drop it to the actual start. To do this, first click on the hand symbol indicated on Route Creation Five. Then point your mouse cursor at the 'A' and click and hold down the left mouse button. Whilst holding the button down, move the 'A' around the screen using your mouse. As you move the mouse around you will note that the route changes to follow. Once you have located the correct start position release the mouse button.

To change the other destination points zoom out on the map using the mouse roller or the zoom scroll bar on the screen until you can see them and then repeat the above.

You can further fine tune the map by grabbing the

route line at any point and dragging it around the map. If you hover your mouse cursor over the route line you will note that a small white circle appears with the words 'Drag to change route' (see Route Creation Five). The mouse icon will also change to a pointing finger. In the same way as moving the destination points you can grab the circle (by left clicking and holding the button down) and drag it around the map. If you hover the circle at any point on the map, after a couple of seconds you will see that the route line changes to show you what the route would look like if you were to drop the circle there. (Essential you are telling Google Maps that the route MUST go to the point where the white circle is.) Drag the circle around until you are happy with the route then release the mouse button to drop the circle. It may be that you will have to repeat this process several times at different points along the route in order to get your ideal route.

Please note that there is a limit to the number of drag points you can use on any single route. Therefore, if you have a long route or it is particularly complex you may have to break it into parts and save each one separately.

Once you are happy with the route shown on the map you can name it by clicking on the words 'Untitled map' (see Route Creation Six) and filling in the relevant details on the pop up box. The map will be saved under your 'My Maps' with that title.

Route Creation Six

If you wish to create written directions click on the three vertical dots indicated on Route Creation Six and then select 'Step-by-step directions' from the dropdown list. Copy the directions that appear by clicking (and holding down) your left mouse button at the top of the directions and then pulling the mouse down (still holding the mouse button down) until all the directions are highlighted (you will need to scroll downwards by dragging your mouse down the screen). Once you have all the directions highlighted, release the left mouse button and point the cursor somewhere in the highlighted area. Now click the right mouse button and select 'copy' from the drop down menu.

Having taken a copy of the directions you need to paste them somewhere. Personally I use MS Word. Simply open a blank document, click the right hand mouse button whilst the cursor is somewhere in the document and select paste from the drop down menu.

Now save this document to a convenient location on your computer or a data stick (in a folder called 'cycle routes' or 'end to end route' or similar). Remember to call the file something you can easily recognise, e.g. 'end to end directions – Day 1'. Once saved, you can return to the document at any time to make amendments (if required) and to print.

You should now have a Google My Map and a set of amendable written directions saved.

How to get a route from Google My Maps to a GPS Device

If you also want to create a gpx file of the route for a navigation device then follow the instructions below.

1. If you do not already have the map open then open your web browser and search for 'google my maps' (see Route Creation Seven).

2. On the next screen click

Route Creation Seven

'Open a map' (see Route Creation Eight).

3. Check the tick box next to the map you wish to create the gpx for and click 'Select' (see Route Creation Nine).

4. Click on the 'Share' icon (see Route Creation Ten). On the next screen you can add a name and a description if you have not done so already. If you do so click 'Save'. Otherwise click 'Skip'.

Route Creation Eight

5. On the next screen right click the highlighted URL link and select 'Copy' from the popup menu (see Route Creation Eleven). Then click 'Change' and on the next screen change the access rights to 'Anyone with the link' and click 'Done' (see Route Creation Twelve). This is important otherwise in the next steps you will get an error.

6. Go to **www.gpsvisualizer.com/convert_input? convert_output=gpx** and paste the URL link address where it says 'provide the URL of a file on the Web', tick GPX and click the Convert button (see Route Creation Thirteen).

Route Creation Nine

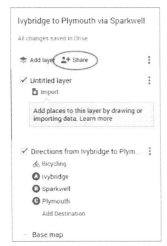

Route Creation Ten

Route Creation Eleven

Route Creation Twelve

NB. If you would like elevation details for your route, before you click Convert click the little arrow by 'add DEM elevation data' and select 'from best available source'.

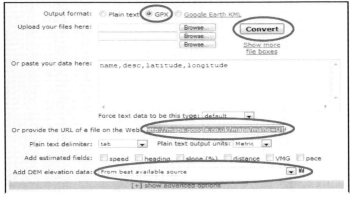

Route Creation Thirteen

7. Once the route has been converted click the download link and save as [filename].gpx (see Route Creation Fourteen). Remember to call the file something more convenient than the name automatically allocated to it, e.g. 'end to end - Day 1' If you forget when you download it then go to the file location and rename it before creating any more routes otherwise you'll never tell them apart.

8. If you have added elevation data you can return to www.gpsvisualiser and under 'Map this data' click 'elevation profile'. This will provide you with a graph of the route profile. You can download this or print it direct. I would advocate downloading it because this will give you the opportunity to manipulate the image if you want to.

You should now have your route saved as a Google My Map with printable route directions and a gpx file ready to upload to your gps unit, using whatever software the manufacturer recommends. I have a Garmin and I copy the files direct to the unit by attaching it via a USB port and using Windows Explorer. There is a GPX folder and I simply copy them into it.

Route Creation Fourteen

End

You've prepared your route, done the training, packed your bags, and managed to get yourself to your chosen start. Now all you have to do is the ride. It is the end, or at least the beginning of the end. You have nothing to do but sit on your bike, point it up (or down) and begin pedalling. And in approximately ¼ million pedal rotations you'll arrive at the finish.

Whilst the pedalling will be hard work at times it is a wonderful feeling to know that it is all you have to do. There is nothing else to distract you from your task and when you reach your destination at the end of each day all you can just collapse. The only multi-tasking you will have to do is pedalling and drinking and/or eating. You can shut down most of your hyperactive brain functions and zone out on the pedal strokes.

My only warnings to you are:

- **Don't overdo it early on**. This counts for the tour as a whole and for each individual day. You have a long way to go and it is better to spread your energy output as evenly as possible. It is very tempting to zip away on day one when you are feeling (relatively) fresh and the adrenaline is pumping but you will pay later. Of course, by the time you get a few days in you might not feel up to overdoing it early on: from day three on it took me about 50 miles to warm up.

- **Watch out for day three.** Apparently this is the worst day. Day one you are on a high. Day two you can feel the effects of day one but you can push through the aches and pains and the niggling tiredness. Day three everything is feeling stiff and your energy is almost as low as your morale – because you still have such a long way to go! I felt quite sick in the morning of day three and found it difficult to get food down – but you have to if not it's a downward spiral. Your 'day three' might come on a different day. But you almost certainly will get one!

- **Break the day up into manageable chunks**. You'll go nuts if you think about the total distance you have to cycle and start counting off the miles. Set your horizons on the next town not the B&B/campsite/hotel/gutter at the end of the day. Long distance cycling is psychological warfare and if you let your guard down when you are tired you will take a pounding. On my trip I had a fantastic early morning session on day two. I rode past Ben Nevis and up through Glen Coe. The late morning session was tougher than I had expected and I was tired with a sore butt by lunchtime. I was feeling quite bad and then I looked at the route and realised just how far I still had to go to reach my B&B. Which was many miles past the part of the entire route that I was least looking forward to – the A82 into Glasgow. And then the devil on my shoulder pointed out that this was just day 2 and I had to do this for another 4 long grueling days (if I managed to get to the end of the day). She then reminded me that I'd feel even worse tomorrow. And the next day. And the next day. And the next day... I felt very low until I managed to wrestle the devil back into her box and fix my concentrate on the next manageable chunk, the next town.
- **Try to keep your concentration** up towards the end of each day. Especially so the further you get into the tour. It is very easy to make mistakes due to tiredness. These can be annoying if you misread your route or deadly if you misread the road. Try caffeine to boost concentration if your system can tolerate it. But beware that too much can make you

sick and remember that you do need to sleep at the end of the day! If you feel your concentration is slipping it's time to take a break and maybe have a cat nap, if you can.

- **Enjoy** yourself. That's why you are doing this!

My End to End

I have set out below an account of my end-to-end as an insight into what the ride experience might be like. I have also included copies of the bloggy sort of emails my wife sent to friends and relatives whilst I was en-route in the Appendix.

Day Zero – Ivybridge to John O'Groats – 1,208 km (750 miles)

The bag was packed (and compressed to make sure it fitted within the hand luggage dimensions), the bike together with my helmet and shoes were sat in a bike shop in Wick (fingers crossed) and I certainly couldn't do any more training now so all I had to do was get up with the alarm, rush around a bit, shout at people to hurry up and drive to the airport.

Bag packed, bike there, alarm, get up, shower, grab bag and drive to airport. I ran through the litany once more and craned my head off the pillow to look at the alarm clock. Another minute had slipped past.

I revised the litany: bag packed, bike there, *go to bloody sleep before the alarm goes off*, get up, shower, grab bag and drive to the airport.

I must have dropped off at some point because the alarm did go off and thanks to a wife much calmer than me I managed to arrive at the airport, on time, with my bag *and* the tickets and passport I had completely forgotten about.

Having never flown internally before I must admit that I was sceptical. Whilst my flights weren't ridiculously cheap they were, nevertheless, cheap and I've not been awash with glowing recommendations for cheap flight deals. We've all heard the horror stories.

I don't quite know what I was expecting when I marched up to the check in desk wearing my early morning scowl but it wasn't a flawless check in and to be told that the flight was scheduled for take-off on time.

Feeling buoyed, and yet strangely cheated, I made my emotional farewells and trudged through to wait for the call to board. As I sat down I risked letting the tension off the restraining strap on my bag, pulled out a book and settled in for a long wait. I was convinced that now the ~~victims~~ passengers we were past the check in and had no one to moan at, the airline would hit us with the bad news, "Flight XYZ1 to Edinburgh has been delayed due to blah blah blah". Still, I had a couple of hours between this flight arriving in Edinburgh and my connector leaving for Wick so I had a bit of time to play... "Would passengers for flight XYZ1 to Edinburgh

please proceed to boarding gate 2. Please have your boarding pass ready for immediate departure."

Gosh! Ok, a bit of poetic license used but the flight did leave bang on time, the attendant was very pleasant and whilst the plane was noisy the flight was short. The connector flight to Wick was also beyond my expectations and the attendant even dished out free drinks and snacks.

So, I was in Wick and it was only just lunchtime! Funny to think it would take me six days to cycle back again. The only downer on the flight was having my butt cream confiscated because the tub was slightly over the size limit (even though it was only half full!). Never mind, Sudocrem ® is widely available and I picked up a fresh supply in Wick.

I must admit to feeling a bit apprehensive as I walked to the bike shop. A couple of days earlier I had phoned to check that my bike had arrived but the person on the other end had such a strong accent that I couldn't quite understand them. It was a bit of a confused conversation, probably because they couldn't understand me either. Anyway, over the last two days the feeling had built that I might have misunderstood and my bike wasn't there. I was *almost* sure, "D'nay fash yourself!" meant, "Don't worry."

As I approached the shop the door was wide open in the early afternoon sunshine. When I got closer the first thing to greet me, just inside the door, was my bike. I was much relieved. And pleased as well because someone had straightened the handlebars and draped my helmet and shoes over them so it was ready to go.

I ventured deeper into the shop to find someone to thank but couldn't find anyone in the eclectic jumble: it had more the feel of an overstuffed second hand shop than a bike shop. After a minute or two I called out but there didn't seem to be anyone around. I wondered whether I should just take the bike but thought that might give the shop keeper a bit of a shock when they came back.

Having just decided to write a note for them the shop keeper appeared, just like in a Mr Benn cartoon. I thanked them for accepting the bike and setting it up for me and after a few initial refusals managed to get them to accept £10 for their troubles. They also let me change into my cycling gear ready for the ride up to John O'Groats, which saved risking arrest by doing it on the High Street. Feeling much cheered I couldn't get the Mr Benn shop keeper image out of my head and wondered if I might step out of the changing room into a strange five minute, costume based adventure.

By the time I had stopped for the third time to readjust my handlebars on the cycle up to John O'Groats my feelings of good cheer had eroded somewhat. I cursed under my breath wondering if I might have to keep doing this all the way to Land's End on the six day, costume based adventure I was actually about to embark on. And now that my sense of relief had passed it suddenly struck me for the first time that my bike might not have been particularly secure sat in the open doorway of an unattended shop. Bloody magic shop keepers!

Cycling past my B&B (about 4 miles south of John O'Groats) I pushed on to John O'Groats to check out the start post. Here I persuaded the attendant photographer (after I had woken him up) to change the date on the post to the next day (when I would be starting). He obliged and I took my start photos then because things wouldn't look so good at 06:00 the next morning. I certainly wouldn't anyway.

Before heading back down the road to the B&B I detoured to Duncansby Head. Despite John O'Groats being the official finishing point (or starting point) of an end to end Duncansby Head is actually the most

North Easterly point so I felt I should roll my rubber to the end of the road.

As I sat on the grass looking out over the Orkney Islands I decided to load the route for day one on the sat nav and follow it to the B&B. This was fairly pointless from a navigation point of view because there was only one road but I just wanted to make sure it was working ok. I switched it on and went to pick 'Day One' from the list of routes. Let's see...menu - click...where to? - click...routes - click...arghh! No bloody routes. Fumble, fumble. Click, click. They must be here somewhere! Click, click. Sweat, sweat. Click, click. Shake, shake. Click, click. Bang, bang!

But no amount of clicking or shaking or banging of the sat nav made them appear: I had forgotten to download them! After hours of painstaking mouse clicking and cursing I had forgotten to download the ✄@%✆ routes.

Now I must admit that I wasn't overly concerned about not having the routes on the sat nav because I had my written route sheets and I was much more familiar with using them. But if my long suffering wife found out I would be in trouble. Firstly, for not having the routes, which was a safety net for her, and secondly for wasting £300 on a tool specifically bought for this trip which was now useless.

So what to do? Confess and try to laugh it off? Or

blag my way through the week by making up little sat nav anecdotes? Fortunately I was in a loving and supportive relationship so my course was clear.

As I spun the pedals on the way to the B&B I started to think up my first anecdote,'…and I ended up in the sea!','…took me the wrong way round the one way system', '…through a field of Aberdeen Anguses!','…and I think they were even more surprised than I was to find me in their swimming pool'. And then it struck me that when I created the routes on-line I had made them public. Which meant that I could download them from anywhere with internet access. The B&B had a website so surely they had an internet connection. All I had to do was beg.

And so it proved. Five minutes of connectivity and the routes were all safely on the sat nav. No one need ever know. And, until now, nobody ever did.

The B&B was very pleasant with great views over sheep covered fields and out across the North Sea. My bike was securely locked up and the hosts were the only ones on the trip who offered to put out some cereal etc for breakfast because I planned to be on the road before they would be up.

Day One – John O'Groats to Fort Augustus – 241.5 km (150 miles)

I was up at 5:00 and forced down 900 ml of protein drink, a brioche and a cereal bar whilst struggling into my kit and gathering various battery powered items that were charging around the room [being charged up rather than hurtling about]. Then, trying to be as quiet as a mouse, I tip toed downstairs and nibbled the breakfast that had been laid out.

Fully engorged I slipped out the door, retrieved my bike from the garage, sent a text to say I was up, and began the 4 mile cycle to the start.

It was ominously quite when I arrived at John O'Groats. I rolled up to the signpost and ceremoniously touched it before sending another text, signalling that I was on my way back home (5:47). There was an eerie light that early in the morning and I set off under the

baleful glare of a seagull perched on the signpost: the only other living thing around. In my mind I substituted a cactus for the signpost and a vulture for the

seagull and imagined tumbleweeds rolling down the desolate road. It was all quite surreal.

As I rolled down the road, past the B&B and on towards Wick, I wondered how long it would be before I passed other end to enders going the other way – nearly there! I didn't have a lot else to think about, my next route instruction was 33 miles away! Quite frankly most of the route instructions on day one were only there to give me some indication that I was moving along. There aren't many route options that far north.

Of course it was a long time before I did pass anyone: it was very early and if they had been that close to the finish the day before they would have pushed on. When I did pass someone I gave them a cheery wave but I'm not sure they really registered it. They had a very fixed expression and looked dead behind the eyes.

I, on the other hand, felt great. My laboriously crammed down breakfast had dropped into my legs and I was remembering to top up the fuel supply regularly as well. And the road was sublime: very gently rolling, good surface, hardly any traffic and fantastic views.

However, I knew from various accounts I had read that two of the major hills of the entire route lay ahead, at Berriedale and Helms Deep [sorry, Helmsdale] respectively. So I appreciated the rolling terrain whilst I could and prepared myself for the worst.

Just over forty miles from the start I began the Berriedale descent. Having seen only one other cyclist all morning I suddenly came upon a number spread out and struggling up the slope. It was like a sticky insect trap for cyclists: they

whizzed into the bottom, all unexpectant, and then had to drag themselves with inexorable cyclist grit through the gloop until they escaped to freedom at the top. And so far only that one I had passed earlier had managed it. The rest could have been there for days for all I knew.

As it happens I seemed to be going the right way for both this hill and the one at Helms Deep. Both were much more severe going north.

I stopped at Helms Deep to see if I could spot Aragorn, Gimli and Legolas but they weren't around,

so I topped up with water at the local convenience store. Bearing in mind that this is one of the few convenience stores on the only main road on this part of the end to end, I was surprised at the funny looks I got in the shop from both the locals and the shop attendant. You would have thought they were used to cyclist stopping to refuel. Or perhaps it was the word 'solicitor' on my cycling kit?

Whatever it was, they palmed me off with some dodgy looking bank notes. It took me nearly five minutes to persuade a Cornish burger van owner to accept one of them a few days later [but then the fiscal system in Cornwall is mainly based on sheep and pasties].

A few miles down the road a magnificent property came into view in the distance, silhouetted against the sea. I thought to stop to take a photo but it was still some way off so decided to wait until I was further down the road. Unfortunately my view then became obscured right up until I was passing the entrance where I discovered it was Dunrobin Castle.

Now I don't know what the significance of the 'Dunrobin' is. It probably means 'head of the Robin Clan' or somesuch. But as I cycled off down the road I couldn't help wondering if it was some poor Scottish joke, like Dunroamin: having stolen a fortune from the neighbouring clans the local leader decided to rub his victims noses in it by building a magnificent home with his ill-gotten gains and labeling it in such a way as to say,

I've fleeced you enough and can't be bothered any more.

I was over a hundred miles into day one before I reached the next milestone - *171[km] L (2nd exit) bfr bridge @ Cromarty Firth – A862.* A change of road! Even with the two major hills the day so far had been flatter  than any 100 mile ride I had ever done and I was feeling relatively fresh. [I've lost the text messages from day one and the first half of day two so I might have actually been feeling fairly crap]. I was almost hoping for some more up and down to relieve the monotony of continuous pedalling. I was far more used to grunt, grunt grunt, freewheel, grunt, grunt, grunt, freewheel, and so on.

The next 25 miles did provide a little more in the way of hills until a prodigious decent to Drumndrochit and the shore of Loch Ness. From there it was back to gently rolling road all the way to the B&B at the southern tip of Loch Ness in Fort Augustus. Here I was treated to a very nice en-suite room with my bike again secure in the garage.

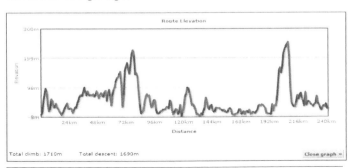

Day Two – Fort Augustus to Kilmarnock – 251.2 km (156 miles)

© 2011 Google – Map

Day Two dawned fair and bright. When the alarm went off at 05:00 I joined it, not quite so fair and definitely not feeling bright. But I was looking forward to today.

My only previous trip to Scotland had been a week's self catering in Spean Bridge, a few miles down the road. It had rained and been overcast for the entire seven days. In fact it was undercast as well: we never saw anything above 100 metres. The views were very much of truncated hills with grey blankets on. Today I would see what we had missed out on. [And I would be very disappointed if all the hills were 100 metres high and completely flat topped]

I managed to get up and on the road a few minutes before my designated 06:00 start time which boosted my mood up to 'slightly grumpy' as I whirred the pedals around in a low gear, trying to ease my aching legs into the day. I had slightly

further to go today, in fact it was my longest scheduled day, and the best thing I could do was to get some steady miles in early on so I wouldn't feel I was playing catch up all day.

From my previous holiday I remembered the road as being mostly flat. But then I was driving, not cycling, and most roads seem fairly flat in a car. If it *was* mostly flat I calculated I could cover the 30 miles or so to Fort William in a couple of hours if I managed the same average speed as yesterday. If I refueled there it would put me in a good position for the short step to the climb up and through Glen Coe.

But I dithered. I was suffering from bladder drip, which I always find takes a while to get under control for the first couple of hours on a ride. Probably a consequence of forcing down all that protein drink, coffee and energy drink first thing to get the system fired up. I certainly wasn't sweating it off in the early morning so the surplus all had to come out somewhere.

And then there were all those great sights and views that I had missed last time around. I felt obliged to take photos of the Aberdeen Angus. I back tracked a few hundred metres to take a shot of Loch Lochy despite telling myself I had already stopped too many times. And I loitered at the Royal Commando memorial at Spean Bridge to take a few shots. I'd seen it before but without the background! (of which my photos do not do justice).

I even stopped to take a picture of the road! I don't know whether it was a sub conscious action, all this picture taking, because my body was feeling achy and it was a good excuse to keep stopping. Consciously I was taking as many photos as possible because I was feeling more than a little guilty that I was getting to enjoy all these views that my wife and I had missed on our holiday, whilst she was stuck at home with the kids and the dogs and the cats.

By the time I rolled into Fort William I was somewhat behind schedule but managed to find somewhere open (it was Sunday) to replenish my water bottles before pedalling on.

Fortunately the stretch to the Glen Coe climb was less inspiring and I managed with only one or two stops before the ascent. The climb itself was pretty easy going, probably because I kept on stopping to take pictures again. One of my cycling 'things' is that I don't

like to stop on hills (unless I fall off). If I want a rest I tell myself I'll have one at the top (by which time of course I don't need one). But I must have stopped half a dozen times to take shots up and down the glen.

At the top I stopped again and sat by the brook gazing down the climb. Glorious. And, in hindsight, the high point of the entire trip. In my head I'd done the hardest cycling of the day and now it was just cycle through the glen, freewheel down to Loch Lomond, skirt Glasgow (okay, I was a bit worried about that) and a short cross country section to Kilmarnock. But for now the sun was shining and I called home to relay my high spirits.

It's amazing how psychology works. Within ten miles of my high I reached one of my lowest points. My expectations of a cruise through the glen were dashed as it continued to grind up and down for mile after mile. In reality it probably didn't but compared to my expectation it did. And because I thought it would be flat I found myself pushing too hard up the hills, trying to make the same speed as if it was flat.

Stupid! Of course the demon was on my shoulder now telling me that I had been too casual. I'd taken my eye off the ball and wasted precious time snapping away like a tourist. [It was only a long way down the road, when I was closer to my destination, that I remembered that I was a bloody tourist and this was meant to be fun and why shouldn't I take some bloody photos and stuck two fingers up to the demon.]

Playing on my mind as well was my water supply. I was very nearly dry and I still had a long way to go to reach Bridge of Orchy, which I hoped was a small settlement and not just a bridge. First off I tried to ration myself and then reasoned the water was doing me no good in the bottle. So I drained the bottle and ploughed on.

Worried about the water and the fact that I was now behind time the demon started telling me just how far I had to go today and then the next day and the next day and the... 'Your legs are tired, your shoulders ache and this road is meant to be flat, not writhing up and down like a hooked eel. And you've still got miles to go just to get to Bridge of Orchy. Where there probably won't be any water. Look, you've only done ½

a kilometre since you last looked. You've still got 90 miles to go and it's nearly midday! Six hours to cover 60 miles. At this rate you won't get there until 21:00. And you're bound to get more tired so you'll slow down. And your sciatica will play up. There's no point reaching for that water bottle, it's empty. Another 200 metres. Is that all! If you get in really late today you'll suffer for it tomorrow. And that will knock on to the next day. And the next day...'

In that state the minutes seem to take hours but eventually I dragged myself up a final climb and dropped into Bridge of Orchy. There was nothing there except a hotel. Time to beg some water.

I locked the bike to a drainpipe and clicked my way into reception. When I asked, most politely, whether it would be possible to fill my water bottles I was curtly informed that there was a tap outside. I clicked back across the wooden floor muttering choice phrases about the legendary warmth of Scottish hospitality. Still cursing I cast about, looking for this secret tap. And there it was, right by the door, with a big sign saying 'free water – please do not disturb reception' [or that was the gist anyway].

I glanced back through the door and waved a feeble apology to the glaring receptionist. I quickly filled my bottles and wheeled the bike round the corner, out of sight, before mixing up my potions.

Relieved to have liquids back on board I managed to dismiss the demon and think a bit more clearly. I realised that I had pushed too hard for the last few miles and as a result had neglected to eat anything. I remedied this by immediately downing an energy bar and promising myself to keep the supply going regularly.

I don't recall much about the next stage but my text from Crainlarich was, 'v. tired. Long way to go...'. So I guess I was tired and felt I still had a long way to go. I think I was suffering from not eating earlier. I know I stopped at the public toilets in Crainlarich to apply a thick greasing of butt cream because that area had been causing some discomfort. I also guess I must have stopped for much longer than I thought because otherwise, calculating from the time of text messages and the physical distances between them, I only managed 8 mph on the next leg.

On the stretch alongside Loch Lomond I recall feeling a lot better, probably as the food started to

kick in, and making up a lot of time by going really fast. My text from Balloch at the southern end of the loch even says, '...very fast road, so went very fast...' But again the timing of texts etc. show that I only managed 12mph. I do recall stopping and buying food at a convenience store and sitting down to methodically chew my way through it, so I might have lost more time than I thought there. It might have been a sub conscious effort to avoid the next bit. The bit I was least looking forward to: negotiating the run into Glasgow on the A82 and managing to come off at the right junction to go over the Erskine Bridge.

I'd devised a route to avoid the A82 as much as possible on the approach to Glasgow (although I had been riding along it for the whole day so far) and in fact only had to ride the 3 miles just before the bridge. But I was still worried about it because the traffic had been getting progressively worse (more of it and more aggressive) the closer we had got to Glasgow and I was thankful to have turned off at Balloch. At one point I even had a charming kid of about 10 hurl a rock at me from a pedestrian bridge crossing the road. Fortunately he was a crap shot – probably pissed.

When I hit the A82 there was no shoulder that I could cycle along. Unfortunately the lanes also seemed particularly narrow and the traffic was very heavy: it was nearly 17:00 and everyone was heading back home after their Sunday afternoon spent soaking up sun and lager on the shores of Loch Lomond.

Having joined the road there was nothing I could do but carry on as fast as possible in the hopes that I could get off before I was knocked off. I charged on purposefully, keeping the cars at bay by force of mind alone. It was taxing but I was managing to deflect even the most wobbly drivers. In a big gear, each pedal rotation was driving me 9 metres closer to the bridge and comparative safety.

I only had a mile to go when the heavens opened and dropped the contents of a small lake on the road. Visibility was suddenly cut down to nothing, with rain bouncing off the tarmac and plumes of spray jetting out from the speeding traffic. I quickly stretched down and switched my rear light on but didn't think it would provide much visibility: I could hardly see the cars in front. The virtual white out didn't slow the traffic though.

A driveway appeared out of the murk and I thankfully pulled off before I got mushed. As I tried to shelter under a small tree I mused that if it rained like this on day four, on the urban stretch through the midlands, I might have a very nervous and uncomfortable day.

The rain left as quickly as it came and after waiting a few minutes for the heavy traffic to clear the surface water from the road I crept out of hiding and sprinted as fast as possible for the slip road to the Erskine Bridge and freedom.

It was a big relief to get off the main road and I felt a big weight lifted. I think the last stretch had been playing on my mind all day, probably why I had been prevaricating, stopping for photos and the like. And with a lighter load I speeded up. For the last leg of my day, from the Erskine Bridge to Kilmarnock, I averaged 15mph, despite it being quite uppy downy [a term you'll only find in the most technical of cycling texts]. But I was still very relieved to get to the B&B. I was proper tired.

As I went through my evening routine I noticed I hadn't eaten all of my food rations, which wouldn't have helped my energy levels. I tried to eat what I could but it was an effort and I was still left with a surfeit. I determined that I would try harder to eat more regularly the next day.

I had developed sciatica during training and in the last two weeks the knee on the other side had started playing up, probably over compensating. Whilst this hadn't been a problem on day 1, I had suffered a number of tweaks today on the steeper hills. So I went to sleep wondering whether I should tackle the Kirkstone Pass, which I had detoured my main road route specifically to climb. It was meant to be the main challenge of the route but I didn't want to jeopardise the whole thing by damaging something in the effort.

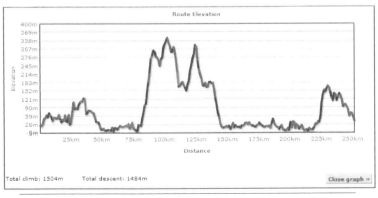

Day Three –Kilmarnock to Kendal– 241.7 km (150 miles)

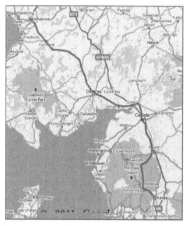

I'd been warned about day 3 by a number of people. It was the day when the cumulative physical effects of the previous two days would kick in with the added physiological weight of knowing that there were more days to come and you could only get more tired. But I was determined to be mentally prepared and tackle the demon the moment he turned up.

This was probably why I was awake at 04:15. It took me longer to get going than the previous two days: I was feeling quite nauseous and it took a long time to get the breakfast potions and bars down. But I was determined to follow through with my pledge of the evening before, so down they went. Fortunately they stayed down as well. Although it was touch and go.

I set off through a very quite but quite grim Kilmarnock and down the B7073 toward the A76 which would take me to Dumfries. From there I'd merge with the A75 which I'd follow to Gretna and the border. But that was 80 miles away.

To be honest I remember very little about the road to Gretna. My text messages don't help much in filling in the gaps either. Apparently I felt crap an hour down the road and only started to feel better near Dumfries, 60 miles and nearly 5 hours into the day.

The road did get very busy after Dumfries and the

right turn into Gretna was a little hairy after the tarmac beyond the rumble strip disappeared on the approach but I arrived safe and sound.

I stopped in Gretna for a Cornish pasty. I should have gone for a Scotch pie because they had no idea how to make a Cornish pasty. Still, I struggled it down, along with an energy bar and a protein bar, resolute to munch my way through my surplus supplies.

After posing for the obligatory photo at the border I headed east to join up with A7 to take me into Carlisle. This was the last photo I took before reaching Tintern Abbey in the Wye Valley of south eastern Wales. This either shows determined riding on my part or a complete lack of photogenic scenery in the 270 miles of England between the two points. I like to think I was very focused.

From Carlisle I joined the A6 and was destined to follow it for the next 100 miles all the way to Chorley, south of Preston. At High Hesket I made the decision to avoid the 25% Kirkstone Pass and stick to the much easier A6 route over Shap Fell. Whilst my sciatica was in abeyance and my knee had not been too bad today I didn't want to take the risk of an injury which might put a stop to the whole trip.

As if to spite me, my chain started playing up a few miles later. There seemed to be too much play in it. I was surprised that the bike shop hadn't recommended a replacement when it had been serviced because it had already done 2,000 hard miles which included over 40,000 metres of vertical climb (an average 100 mile ride in Devon means 2000 metres of climb – and if the organisors want to be nasty it can be double that). 10

speed chains don't seem to last very long, especially if you ride them through all types of weather and down muddy gritty lanes.

I decided that I would stop the next time I saw a bike shop and try to replace it. Although the last one I had seen was in Wick. So I might have to specifically seek one out. Penrith was the next main town so I'd stop there to track one down.

I was doing much better today at eating regularly and my energy level seem quite consistent, even though I could feel general fatigue gnawing away in the back ground. But I still didn't seem to be getting through my full allocation. It was really hard work forcing the bars, gels and drinks down and it was only the thought of feeling worse that focused my mind enough to do it. Even so, my supply wasn't going down that fast and there would be another lot waiting for me at the B&B in Kendal.

I didn't have to seek very hard for a cycle shop in Penrith, there were two on the High Street. The first one didn't have a 10 speed chain in stock and the second wanted to charge me £43.00. Having only fitted one a couple of months before which had cost me about £17.00, I decided I would ride on to Kendal and see if I could find a cheaper one there.

The climb over Shap Fell was long but not too steep. I think the steepest part was about 10%. This was not a worry for me on a light weight bike with only one bag. It would be much more of a problem for a fully laden camper/tourer. The slope on the other side was more severe (probably about 13-15% near the top) and provided me with one of my highest speeds on the tour, about 42 mph. If I had been brave and felt more alert it could have been faster but having missed the Kirkstone Pass to avoid an injury I didn't want to get one here by over cooking it into a corner.

I was approaching Kendal from a different

direction to my route sheet so had to stay alert to find my B&B. I knew that the final half mile or so to the actual B&B would be the same as my planned route so I switched on the sat nav and waited to pick up the pink highlighted route. Sure enough it didn't let me down and took me almost to the door.

The room was en-suite with a choice of beds! It also had a radiator and, despite it being July, I turned it on to dry out my kit, after cleaning it in the shower using the grape treading technique.

I decided I was too tired to go looking for a chain, and everywhere would be closed anyway, so I settled into my evening routine of charging things up, eating and setting out everything in nice piles for a quick re-pack of the bag and pockets in the morning. I'm never very with it first thing and with three long days in the saddle behind me I needed all the help I could get.

Despite my best efforts my bow wave of energy bars and gels had grown larger and was now causing problems with both bag space and weight. The gels in particular were quite heavy and the surplus probably weighed a couple of kilos. I was loath to dump them because they cost a lot of money and I'm tight. Perhaps if I met any cyclists the next day I could try giving them away. Although, other than the first day, I couldn't recall seeing any other cyclists. I suppose 'A' roads aren't all that popular.

I was feeling pretty shattered but happy to have

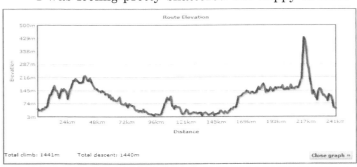

got through the dreaded Day 3. In theory things shouldn't get any worse now. Although I wasn't particularly looking forward to tomorrow, not from a fatigue point of view, just because my only image of the area was the mutli-coloured splat of spaghetti over several pages of the road atlas.

Day Four – Kendal to Shrewsbury – 206.4 km (128 miles)

I got up with the alarm and peered out of the window to see if the forecasted rain had arrived. Fortunately not. Hopefully it would hold off for a while: I don't mind cycling in the rain but I hate starting out in the rain.

Each day I was feeling more tired at the start and finding it harder to concentrate on my morning routine. Fortunately I was in the habit of setting out everything in logical piles the night before so I could try and rely on my automatic pilot. First, make strong coffee. Then start eating everything in pile one and rubbing items from pile two into sore parts. Mustn't mix them up. Then gather the charging electrical items and pack piles three to six into the bag, in that order. Finally dress in the clothes in pile seven, pick up the bag and leave as quietly as possible. Simple.

But it still took me 46 minutes! I know this because the alarm was set for 05:00 and I texted to announce my departure at 05:46. Apparently my legs were very stiff. Never mind. Only today to go and then it will be the penultimate day. [This sounds much better than, 'I'm knackered and I'm only halfway there!']

By now I was regularly feeling tired, achy, nauseous and feeble in the mornings. I had already learnt that I just needed to keep plodding on, eating what I could (and then forcing down a little more) and after about 100km I would start to feel better. It helped enormously with the mental to know that this was a norm.

Initially the road was quiet, with just the odd lorry thundering past, but it started to wake up around 07:30 and by the time I pulled off the A6 into Garstang at 08:30 it was getting busy.

I got a lot of strange looks and the odd unintelligible but supposedly witty comment from the school kids congealing around the bus stops and as I headed into town hoping to find somewhere to re-fuel.

I replied to a couple of texts whilst I took a well earned break scoffing a bacon sandwich and a bag of crisps. I waved cheerily to the school bus as it passed thinking that, despite the aches and pains, I was going to have a more endurable day than them.

The route sheet was going to get a bit trickier from here on in: I was entering the land of the wiggly multi coloured roads. So far today I had been cycling in a bit of a daze but knew I would have to wake up and start concentrating now. So I sucked down a caffeine gel and set off back to the A6.

I don't remember much of the next few hours. I was obviously too intent on the road to take much notice of anything else. My texts home were merely town names, so no prompts there either. I can say that the area was nowhere near as built up or busy as the road atlas had led me to believe. Yes, there were a lot of large lorries and juggernauts on the major roads but they were helping to drag me along. And whilst I seemed to be cycling on wet roads nearly all the time it was yet to rain on me. In fact, whenever I climbed to the top of a hill I could see showers dotted all around but so far I was leading a charmed life, slipping between them.

Around 13:00 I got lost. I must have taken a wrong turn somewhere and ended up pointing down the wrong road. I turned on the Sat Nav for help. It whirred away, calculating the route and told me I was lost. Thanks! It told me to U-Turn or recalculate the route. Well I didn't want to go backwards so I asked it to recalculate. Whir, whir, beep – nice pink line stretching out before me. Great!

I followed the pink line for a couple of miles growing more and more uneasy as it was heading due west not south. After another mile I stopped and zoomed out on the map. The sat nav was taking me to Chester and then dog legging south. That was miles extra!

Never having used a sat nav before, I assumed that when you asked it to recalculate it would take you to the closest point on your original route, after all that is what I would do if I had a map. What it actually did was redo the entire route, from the point I was at to the finish point, providing the quickest, but not necessarily the most direct, route. So the sat nav had re-routed me via Chester, which was probably quicker if you were in a car but not on a bike.

I have now learnt never to ask the sat nav to recalculate a route if I get lost [unless I just want to get to the end and am not bothered about how I get there, i.e. I don't have to reach certain check in points like on an Audax ride]. I just zoom out on the map and manually find my way back to the pink line.

But at that point I didn't realise what it had done and, having heard all the horror stories, just assumed the sat nav had freaked out completely. So I abandoned the sat nav and headed off on as southerly a route as I could manage in the hopes of picking up signs to the major towns on my written route sheet.

Sure enough I was soon back on route and trundling through the miles quite quickly. Before I knew it I was through the 'urban sprawl', that never really was, and charging towards Shrewsbury. Today was my shortest day and I reached the B&B by about 16:30.

I had quite a long conversation with the landlady about my bike. Her idea of secure parking was to chain it to a post. I wasn't entirely enamoured with the idea, especially as the post in question was only five foot tall with no loops or securing points: so all you had to do was lift the whole bike up and slip the chain off the top! Eventually she capitulated and let me lock it in the laundry room. She even gave me a key when I said I would be off before six.

The B&B was the worst on the route: surly host, no en-suite and a poky room next to the toilet. I got a shower in quickly before any other ~~victims~~ guests turned up and barricaded myself in my room.

The room did have a television though and I was amazed to see that the local County Show had been all but washed out in the rain. In fact the news was all about how much it had rained in the area all day. This was a big surprise to me because I had managed to cycle 130 miles or so and only get showered on once. I must have been doing something right – maybe it was because I was riding for charity, mate.

I tried to capitalise on my short day and get to sleep early. But the B&B was right next to a busy road with a Mc Donald's and a Pizza Hut opposite, both with a continuous stream of overly noisy customers.

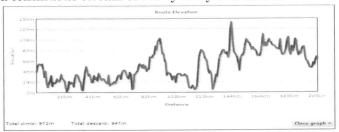

Day Five – Shrewsbury to Taunton – 245.1 km (152 miles)

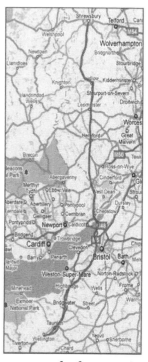

The radio woke me from a dead sleep with rap music and I groggily swung my legs over the side of the bed. I couldn't afford to dwell in the warmth because there was no snooze on the alarm. I stumbled about, trying not to make too much noise but couldn't seem to co-ordinate myself. I sat back down and rubbed my face in an attempt to wake up.

It was only then I realised that the rap music was still playing and the reason I was stumbling about so much was because it was dark. A car door slammed shut outside, slightly muffling the rap music, there was a squeal of tyres and the music receded into the distance at speed, accompanied by a roaring engine.

At this point my brain reminded me that I didn't have a radio alarm on my wrist watch. And it certainly wouldn't be playing rap if I did, unless Radio 2 had changed dramatically in the last few days. I checked said watch and it showed me it was 01:30. Time to go back to sleep!

When the alarm did go off I think I might have felt even worse. And there was no kettle so I couldn't have a nice 'wake me up' coffee. I had to rely on a caffeine gel. Not very palatable.

Despite trying to get out as quickly as possible I

was still a minute slower than the day before! Must be getting more tired. Still, only today to go and then it will be the final day. Good as there really.

I creaked my way back onto the A49, which I had been following since Winwick, about 65 miles back, and was destined to continue along until just after Hereford, a further 56 miles down the road. Hopefully by then my body would have warmed up and I'd feel more like tackling the other 100 miles or so.

The area I was cycling through was much more countrified than the day before and the A49 bypassed most of the towns along the route. As usual in the early morning, I was not feeling too good and was loath to turn off the road in search of refuelling stops: I just wanted to plod on, churning the pedals around waiting to feel a bit more alive. But after 3½ hours or so I was running dry and knew that I would have to find somewhere to stop in Hereford.

As luck would have it I came across a roadside burger van a few miles before Hereford. A huge bacon bap and a large mug of coffee quickly rejuvenated me, both physically and mentally.

After Hereford I left the A49 for the A466 to cross the Welsh border and on to Monmouth. The route from here to Chepstow wound through the Wye Valley and proved to be one of the best stretches of the tour. It was very scenic, peaceful after the busy main road and was very easy riding.

From just south of Monmouth the border follows the River Wye so every time I crossed the river I changed country. Fortunately there was no border control or I would have been there all day!

Despite it's charms the Wye Valley is lacks re-fuelling places and I was running on dry again by the time I reached Tintern Abbey. It was a warm day and the place was fairly busy as I cruised up to the gift shop. When I made my way inside there was a bit of a

gathering around the chilled drinks cabinet where a group were deciding what to buy. Scanning the cabinet through a gap between the throng I spotted that there were hardly any bottles of water left. So with a brisk, 'Excuse me!' I reached through the press of bodies and grabbed the last 4 500ml bottles of water in the cabinet. They cost a fortune but at that stage I was more than happy to pay.

I was pleased to have filled my bottles before Chepstow because it meant I didn't have to side-track into the town: having recently visited Chepstow Castle with my family I remember it as being very hilly. All I had to do was cruise down to the bridge and trundle across.

The trouble was I was in urgent need of a wee and everywhere was a bit urban. There didn't seem to be anywhere to hide myself away. In the end, in desperation, I did a Paula Radcliffe and squatted down behind my bike in a layby, pretending to fiddle with the gears, with one leg of my shorts pulled up and a gush of wee hitting the tarmac. Not very dignified but at least there wasn't a TV camera

broadcasting my shame to millions around the world.

The cycle track on the bridge is a separate structure hanging of the side of the main bridge so you do not have to compete with the traffic in any way. Having said that I was surprised when a motorbike came speeding past. I'm not sure if they were supposed to be on the cycle track mind.

What you might have to battle with is the wind. The bridge is very exposed. In fact a couple of hundred metres on to the bridge there is a sign showing that the bridge is closed to cyclist in high winds with a gate ready to be locked to prevent entry. It was open on the day I went over – the idea of having to re-route via Gloucester [an extra 55 miles or so] didn't bear thinking about. If I was planning to cross the bridge again I would make sure I had the 24/7 helpline number [01454 635 060 at time of publication] to check if the bridge was open long before I got to it so I could re-route early if required. [This is a pre-recorded service but if you wait until the end of the message you can speak to the Supervisor on duty, apparently.]

The A403 from the bridge to Avonmouth was badly cut up when I cycled it. It takes a major pounding by very large trucks as they thunder up and down the road.

I turned off onto the A4 Parkway somewhere around Avonmouth, which follows the River Avon upstream into Bristol. This road was also very busy and I really had to try and keep my concentration up. On some stretches of the road there was a cycle lane but it would keep disappearing, forcing you out into the dual carriage way. The problem was that a lot of the road was too narrow for two lanes and a cycle lane. Quite frankly with the number of heavy lorries using the road it wasn't really even wide enough for two lanes. But they put a cycle lane in where they could, sometimes with cars parked on it when the road passed through residential areas. It would have been safer if they hadn't bothered. A cycle lane tends to encourage motorised road users to think it is perfectly safe for the cyclist if they drive right up to the line. Sadly cycle paths are rarely as wide as they should be, often with obstacles such as storm drain covers taking up the entire width in parts. So other road user are not expecting you to cycle close to the line or even have to cross the demarcation to avoid such obstacles. But don't get me started on cycle lanes...you haven't got the patience.

I was grateful to turn off the A4, even if it meant a stiff climb up to the iconic Clifton Suspension Bridge, the engineering marvel of its day, designed by Isambard Kingdom Brunel in 1831. [Due to a number of complications the bridge was only completed in 1864, after (and in memorial to) Brunel's death.] The bridge is more photogenic from a distance but I didn't intend to descend the hill again so risked life and limb by standing in the middle of the road to take a picture.

I had nabbed the next bit of my route from somebody else who obviously had local knowledge. It took me off the public road and had me cycling through Ashton Court Estate, which was nice.

After re-fuelling at a small supermarket on Long Ashton Road I headed, via very minor lanes, towards the A38 which would take me all the way to Taunton. Sadly I suffered a momentary lapse of concentration.

I managed: *174.3 Flw Long Ashton Rd (-> Wstrn Rd) 2.5 km whr L - Wild Country Ln (if train - too far).* But on the tiny lanes I thought I had done: *176.5 s/o @ staggered X onto*

Hobbs Lane but it must have been a cross that was unmarked on the bikely map. So when I hit the A370 where I should have gone over the staggered X onto Hobbs Lane I thought it was: *177.3 R @ X onto A38.* So I turned right down the busy road which I thought was the A38 but was actually the A370.

It took me seven minutes to realise I had gone wrong. I know this because I texted home at 15:23 on joining the 'A38' to say I was near Bristol Airport, which was meant to be 2½ miles down the road. At 15:30 I was on the phone saying I was lost!

In my very fatigued state I couldn't work out where I had gone wrong and it was only later that I pieced things together. I had tried the sat nav but came up against the same problem as the previous day: I rerouted and it was now sending me via Weston Super Mare [of course the real problem was that I didn't know how to use it!]. So I called home and tried to describe where I was and my wife got out the road atlas and gave me directions to get back to the A38.

The directions were entirely correct but my

interpretation of them on the ground wasn't. I ended up going round in circles a couple of times and called home again. This time I worked out where I was going wrong and was soon on a very direct road to the A38 and back on route.

Now, if I had had a map with me I would have been able to see very easily how to get to the A38. But that was the choice I had made at the beginning and now I would have to live with it. My navigation team had done a wonderful job but the whole episode had cost me nearly an hour and added an extra 20 km to my day. Fortunately all I had to do was follow the A38 until near the finish so I wouldn't have to keep mentally adding the extra distance to my route directions.

The next part of the route was very flat and I pushed hard trying to make up some of the lost time. I must have zoned out because all I can remember is wondering why the road always seemed to get busier whenever I approached a junction feeding onto the M5. I could understand it potentially being busier *after* the junction, if fresh traffic had joined the road, but couldn't work out why it was busier before. I imagine it was a case of sod's law, like you always notice that the other queue is moving faster, and it only seemed busier near the junction because I was more aware of it (because I had to avoid it). But in my fogged state it just kept rumbling through my mind, over and over, because my brain was too tired to process it.

Despite my fatigue my energy levels were pretty good. My appetite had finally caught up with me and I had made significant inroads into the pile of surplus energy bars and gels today. It felt very strange: my body was feeling really tired, beaten and bashed but I had loads of energy and could easily keep the pedals spinning around, even though I felt like crawling off the bike for a sleep. [At one point I even speculated that if I just had to cycle home (about 100 miles down the road) and not to Land's End, I could probably just push on and not stop at all.] Thus I managed to keep up a good constant speed right to the finish at the B&B.

Having said that, the last few miles are literally a blur in my mind. My concentration had gone almost completely and the last bit was down some tiny lanes with a number of turns and junctions. I knew I wasn't really up to it and was at risk of becoming completely lost in the lanes. If I did it was highly unlikely that the home navigation team would be able to save me from the tangle using a road atlas. So I switched on the sat nav. It showed me that I was on route with a lovely pink line for me to follow. So I followed it.

I knew fairly soon that it was not taking me in by the route I had programmed. There were a couple of junctions that I had looked at in detail using the satellite view on Google map and the sat nav was bypassing them completely. But, too exhausted to do anything else, I blindly followed the pink line. I'd been mulling over in my mind why the sat nav had been sending me by strange routes and the penny had finally dropped that when I asked it to rerouted it wasn't taking me back to my original route but just getting me to the finish. At least I hoped so.

I hit the lanes. But they weren't the lanes I had planned. Spin on. Twist, twist, turn, turn. Deeper and deeper into the spiders web. It was probably a good thing I was so tired, otherwise I would have worried more.

Hours later [it was probably a few minutes at most] I came to a junction I did recognise as part of my route. And then, a few hundred metres down the road, the B&B. More like a country mansion!

I scrolled through the bike computer menu: 265 km (165 miles) and an average speed of 23.4 kph (14.5 mph). By far the longest day. But only one more to go!

I checked into my suite [yes, suite] and collapsed

in my lounge and watched the sheep through the window whilst I decided which bed to sleep in. Life is full of tough decisions.

When I had planned the trip I had envisage that each day I would find a local pub or similar to eat an evening meal at, although this never happened. This B&B was about 4 miles out of Taunton and when planning I didn't think I would want an extra 8 mile round trip just to eat. So I had booked an evening meal at the B&B. Let me tell you that after a week of energy bars, protein shakes and the odd bacon roll, a pasta bake, salad and glass of wine finished off with an apple crumble and custard was like nectar from the gods. The only shame was that I couldn't pack it all in. And this suite and evening meal combined had only cost £30. Bargain!

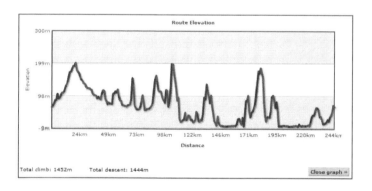

Day Six – Taunton to Land's End – 234.3 km (146 miles)

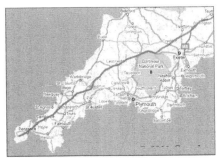

I was slow of the mark for the final day. Every other day I had managed to slip away a few minutes before the planned 06:00 but today I was uncannily precise: my 'off we go' text was timed at 06:00:01.

I was clearly distracted early on because I sent a second text within a few minutes and another half an hour later announcing I was back in my home county of Devon. Only two counties to go! It was just a shame that there probably aren't another two counties in the country with a greater distance to traverse them.

The early morning was a complete misery. Maybe it was because it was the final day and I just wanted to get down the road. Or maybe I just had 750 miles in my legs already and could have done with some more sleep.

I had worked out that if I managed the same speed as the day before I could be finishing by 18:00 but I just couldn't seem to push the pedals around. Probably because the road was rolling up and down much more than it had been over the last few days, making the load on the back feel like lead.

Psychologically things took a major plummet around Bickleigh. I was cutting through small lanes on a local Audax route which would take me to Whiddon Down and the A30. The Audax route kept to the lanes but I remembered it as quite hilly so when I planned this section of the route I had decided to divert to the main road from Bickleigh to Crediton: I reasoned that whilst it would be further to cycle it would be much flatter, being a main road.

I had selected the shortest route possible from the Audax route to Bickleigh. Unfortunately on Google map there was no way to tell it was a 25% hill. Having been up nothing steeper than 13% all week it was a severe shock to the system. Now the one good thing about really steep hills is that they aren't very long because they tackle the hill by a very direct route. But this one seemed to drag on forever. As I rounded each bend I was sure I would see the top, only to see the hill ramping up to the next bend. In Devon they always say there are three tops to any hill: where you think the top is, where you hope the top is and finally where the actual top is. I think this one must have had at least seven tops.

When I finally dragged myself over the top to plunge down the other side into Bickleigh I managed a rueful smile. 'Oh well,' I thought, 'that's Devon for you – never take a direct route it'll only mean hills. But it will be worth it to be able to take the main road and avoid all those other hills.'

But when I turned onto the A3072 to Crediton it just went up and up and up at 15% without end. I was going really slowly now, my legs being shredded by the hills after so much relative flat along the rest of the route from John O'Groats. And when I reached the top the road still seemed to be bucking like a rollercoaster, but that was probably bad mental and fatigue.

When I finally rolled into Crediton I had been on

Total climb: 2070m   Total descent: 2075m   Close graph »

the road for nearly 3 hours and covered only 50 km, which works out about 10½ mph. A far cry from yesterday's 14½ mph. By the time I dragged myself a further 10 miles to Whiddon Down my average speed had dropped to 10 mph and I called home to adjust my eta. If I maintained this speed till the end it would take me another 10½ hours, plus any stoppage time. I hoped the A30 would be faster and guestimated a finish time of 21:00.

The initial few miles on the A30 had me chugging up and down hills but they were much smoother in their profile. Not the short sharp jagged peaks of the lanes but much longer, gentler drags which were much easier on my tired legs because I could settle into the rhythm of each hill. And once I passed Okehampton there was a gloriously long gradual decent which seemed to go on for mile after mile. My speed since joining the A30 had increased significantly and I began to think that I might still be able to finish before my originally scheduled 20:00.

My main concerns for the next few hours were tedium and refueling. My route sheet could have finished at 67 km with: *follow A30 till Land's End.* I had put in a few towns along the way merely to give some impression of progress. In retrospect I should have put in more.

The A30 bypasses all the towns along its route so

to refuel I would have to side-track off the road. With my poor start to the day weighing heavily on my mind I was loath to do this and kept pushing on, trying to make up time. But, like passing services on the motorway when you're low on fuel, you then have to make it to the next one before you run out or you're stuffed. At one point I had drained both my water bottles and had been running dry for half an hour and the next town was still some miles down the road. Thirst was really biting now and I knew I was getting badly dehydrated.

I was starting to think I would have to climb over the barrier at the next industrial unit the road passed and beg water from the first business I came to when I spotted a roadside café in a layby at the bottom of a long drop. Whilst it was annoying having to brake from 40 mph and lose all that lovely momentum I was very relived to stop.

I had a bit of banter with the owner over a Scottish bank note but I think it was friendly because he gave me the most bumper bacon sandwich I think I have ever eaten. I can't even remember where this was but it might have been around Bodmin because there was a text from there [which just read – 'Bodmin'].

By my next stop, a couple of hours down the road, I was able to get a good estimate on my final eta at Land's End, based on my progress along the A30, and phone home to let the collection party know I would probably be there by 19:30 but could arrive by 19:00 if I got some kind of adrenaline rush near the end. I shouldn't have worried, the welcoming committee were already on the road and would try and find me on the A30.

Much buoyed I remounted and sped off down the road. I was looking forward to seeing my wife and kids again. It had only been 6 days but felt like a lot longer.

I was also looking forward to getting rid of my bag.

Half an hour later the cavalry arrived, tooted on the way past and waited in the next layby. Much joy and hugs. Quick chat. Dumped bag in the boot and continued.

A word of warning here. I was prepared for the difference in the handling of my bike when I put the bag on. I was not prepared for the difference when it came off. My body must have got so used to compensating for the extra weight that when I set off I almost pulled myself over and then overcompensated the other way. So I wobbled precariously as I set off and it took a while to settle into things again. It felt a bit like when you've been on a boat for a long time and then come ashore: the land seems to bob up and down whilst the boat had become quite stable.

I practically flew up the next hill.

The support car [gosh, that sounded good!] played leap frog with me, hopping from layby to layby. My wife took some photos but I had to slow down to a virtual standstill before she managed get me in shot properly. It wasn't easy trying to maintain a speedy looking tuck at ½ mph with cars zipping past my right shoulder I can assure you.

After a while the support car disappeared. I was

later to discover that this was for a toilet break. They caught up with me again about an hour later when I was only 4 miles from the finish. Fortunately I hadn't punctured seeing as my repair kit was in my bag in the boot of the car!

Despite the climb in the last few miles I was feeling on a high. I bent over the bars and sprinted the last half mile or so and entered Land's End at speed. But I wasn't sure where to go and there were no directions to the famous signpost. Or if there were they weren't obvious to a fatigued cyclist. I ended up crossing the car park and then having to get off my bike and walk down some steps before remounting to cycle the last few metres to the end. Which was a bit of a shame after cycling nearly 900 miles.

Anyway, the obligatory photos were taken and then it off to Mc Donald's for a celebration supper [kids' idea not mine].

Aftermath

Originally I had planned a whole weekend for recovery from the ride. Funnily enough I didn't need the weekend. For the next few days I felt fine: a little tired, yes, but really ok. And then suddenly, about five days after the finish, it hit me like a rock. I was absolutely exhausted and it took me a couple of days off work and the weekend to get back to the merely tired state I had felt just after the trip.

I have no idea why this happened or even whether it is a normal thing. Perhaps you run on adrenaline for a few days. Or maybe it just takes your body a little while to realise that it doesn't have to push itself so hard anymore. I have heard it take the body two weeks to fully recover from a marathon, so goodness know how long it takes to fully recover from a 900 mile cycle. Just don't plan to catch up on missed chores or work when you get back because you might not be up to it.

The Bitter End

You've worked hard, endured exhaustion, battled lactic acid burn and probably have a boil or two in uncomfortable places. What's kept you going for the last two days is getting back to your loved ones, friends and colleagues. More specifically basking a little in the awe and admiration everyone is bound to hold you in. If you've made your effort for charity (even if only as an excuse) all the better and the more you deserve it. You've earned your bragging rights. Now it's time to cash in.

Sadly it doesn't work that way. Once you've completed your end to end it seems everyone has done it, or at least know someone's granny who did it faster than you on a 1920's fixed wheel, 25 kg bike with 30 kgs of equipment and a baby in the handle bar basket whilst wearing a floor length heavy black velvet dress.

Almost inevitably, just after you finish, your local paper will run a story about an amputee (who tragically lost their leg whilst rescuing a tiny baby in a combine harvester/picnic based disaster) who has just completed an unsupported hop around the world, barefoot, to raise money for orphaned kittens. If your bragging has become intolerable do not be surprised to find that a colleague has accidentally left this open on your desk. Don't let this deter you.

Honestly, this is the end

For those who have read the book:

If you've slogged all the way through the book to here then well done: you have proven that you have the endurance and dogged determination to endure your way through just about anything. A mere end to end will hold no fears for you. Set forth on your path with confidence.

*For those who are in the shop deciding to buy [did you see what I did there – positive action reinforcement, not 'deciding **whether** to buy'] and have flicked to the end to see what sort of conclusion has been reached:*

You now have all the answers you need to plan and complete that Land's End to John O'Groats [or vice versa] ride you've always talked about doing but never got around to. You can now plan, train for and ride your route with confidence. You no longer have any excuses. Put a cross on the calendar and start planning!

Appendix

Copy of Blog created by Wife

Writing in italics are verbatim copies of text messages sent

Sadly the blog for day one and the first half of day 2 have been lost forever. So we begin with…

Day Two, Fort Augustus to Kilmarnock (251 km)

12:11 *Bridge of Orchy.* Making good time - Go Roy!

13:21 *Crainlarich. V tired. Long way to go…*

14:16 *Invergulas*

15:56 *Balloch. Very busy past Loch Lomond – very fast road, so went very fast but felt strain in knee. Everyone returning from their day out in the country.*

16:45 *Erskine Bridge across the Clyde in Glasgow –* Sat nav determined to tell Roy he was going the wrong way, you know what they are like – worse than the wife! *Dual carriage way very busy. Heaven's opened – loads of rain and spray from the road. Pulled over and sheltered under a tree in someone's garden. Let's hope the same thing doesn't happen on Day 4 in the built up area. Will be a very long day otherwise.*

17:21 *Moss Road – closed, but still went through…yes, cyclists are responsible road users…..*

18:50 *Kilmarnock* (one and a half hours ahead of scheduled time). *Recognised B&B on the ring road from the 3 windows at the top in the photo. Saved 1.5 miles* (who's counting?) *Room is ensuite – which is all you could say about it!*

Challenge today – cramming down the calories, just don't want to eat, so has become a mechanical process.

Running total: 310 miles so far, and one third of the way through.....

Day Three, Kilmarnock to Kendal (241 km)

To go or not to go through the Kirkstone Pass????? We will know by the end of today......

04:15 *Awake so decided to leave early...*
05:26 *Off to invade England*
06:34 *Feel crap. Crummoch*
07:02 *New Cumnock*
07:51 *Kirkconnel*
09:04 *Thornhill*
10:10 *Dumfries (or thick chips). Still feel a bit sick but it has taken this long to get into the ride and start to feel okay – 96 km in.*
12:01 *Gretna No propositions yet...* (Thank god, mind you, a good looking chap in lycra.....I'm worried.....)
12:18 *England!* One country down, one to go! 620 km and counting.....

Okay – some summary stats: Roy has cycled through 7 map pages and the total sponsorship currently stands at £660. Go Roy!

For those of you who have queried the clash with the Tour de France...no, not bad planning, first week is usually quiet anyway - all happens in the mountains apparently – and I have set the recorder anyway. Also, Roy wanted to deflect the media attention away from his own exploits, you know what the paparazzi are like.... I don't think Lance feels threatened..... Interestingly, none of the expert panel in Roy's cycling magazine listed Lance in the top 5, so....controversial??? What do we say about that? Watch this space, I guess. No doubt, this will become compulsory viewing from Friday. Anyone want to hold a sweepstake on who wins....trip to the US maybe...

If anyone wants to text Roy to keep his spirits up - goodness knows he needs all the support he can get, especially to get through day 3 - his mobile number is ***** ******. Apparently, this is the equivalent for getting through the 13th mile in a marathon. Get through that, and you know you can make it...(Does anyone know where I can hire any devils with tridents to run alongside.)

Next update tomorrow...

Day Three, continued

14:10   *A6 nr high Heskit. Made decision to avoid the Kirkstone Pass – knee not up to it and don't want to risk the whole journey. Still tweaking on 5-6% hills – Kirkstone Pass is 25%. Will have to save up that challenge up for another day and possibly climb it from all three approaches.* Is this man mad? No, don't answer that question.....

16:19   *Shap. Bike chain is wearing and rubbing – stopped at bike store to change but too expensive £43.* Roy paid £17 I think before he left. *Thought things were cheaper up north...Chain will make it but it is the damage it may be doing to the other parts...Hoping to get to Kendall before 5:00 and possibly change it there.*

16:52   *Top of Shap Fell. Same height as Kirkstone but much easier....*

17:35   *Kendall – End of day three and half way there! (Stuck with old chain...)*

B&B – *choice of two beds to sleep in, ensuite, kettle, TV and a radiator to dry clothes* (my, what luxury, and in the height of summer). *Turned radiator on but now feeling fairly warm and stuffy. Need to turn it off before go to sleep. Have been drying clothes in the window up to now.*

Sounded exhausted on the phone, obviously taking its toll, but fortunately, did have a good night's sleep – nodded off shortly after our phone call around 9:00 leaving the light on and still holding the phone. Woke up realising that he must have fallen asleep type of thing. Alarm woke him this morning which makes a refreshing change. So, sleep is catching up with him.

Day Four, Kendal to Shrewsbury (206 km)

A shorter distance but through built up area of Lancaster, Preston et al on fast roads. Let's hope the rain stays away.

05:46   *Here we go. Legs v stiff*

07:19   *Dry at present* (bucketing it down in Ivybridge...)

07:22   *Lancaster. Only battles are the odd hill and the sat nav..*

07:40   Phone call eating a pepperami. Breakfast consisted of a brunch bar, a brioche and protein drink – all part of the supplies that he posted to each B&B. Now only eating when hungry – cures the sickness/nausea but not good for getting down energy. Is now building a supply of protein and energy bars - quite heavy but at £1 each is loathe to throw them away. Suggested that he gives them away to other cyclists as a random act of kindness....Used the sat nav through Lancaster but will turn it off now. Will turn it on again in Preston. Glad to report that Roy sounded fairly chirpy at this stage.

08:30   *Garstang. Had text from Anne and Rob. Bacon sandwich.* (Wow, that's clever, how did you do that?) ....Meanwhile, I was dropping off a ladybird and dinosaur to school in the rain.

08:47   *Fed and watered. Back on the road.* (Oh, I see what you mean now...you didn't actually text him a sandwich...)

09:49 *Preston*

10:57 *Wigan*

11:33 *Gmlbourne* (Spelling? Does anyone have any clues where he is? Oh, just checked the route – he means Golborne, I think....He does know where he's going, right...no worries, he did pack a compass. Yeah, just head south Roy and then in a westerly direction....Meet you at Land's End...)

So, progress continues. Will be two thirds of the way through by tonight, and the sponsorship is growing, now over £700. Wouldn't it be nice if we could get this up to £900 in total to equate to £1 per mile...Do any of you have any friends...I'm out of options...

More tomorrow....thanks guys.

Day Four, continued...

Oh boy, I must have jinxed Roy, or even I have powers I do not know I have....Or maybe it's Piers' fault, he called about this time....

c13:00 Receive phone call – Roy is lost! Sat nav has let him down and heading out on A56 to Chester. Eventually, Roy overrides sat nav, gets out compass and cuts across country on B roads and...

14:03 *On route, Tarpoley*

14:54 *Whitchurch*

15:28 *Weeing. 20 miles to go.* (Well, we did wonder how this was done...rumour has it he finds discreet farm tracks...Is weeing quite often – every 45 mins apparently - possibly because of the protein. Sue (the doctor in this group) can put us straight on this.

17:22 Shrewsbury (after a shower) Day four

complete! Made good time – huge tail wind. Terrain not hard, surprisingly flat – long, straight Roman roads. Juggernauts really do blast you along - like a hand stretching out and dragging you.

Not feeling as tired as he thought, possibly because he is stopping a lot more than anticipated. Knee is fine – seems it was worse on day one. Does kick in after about 100 miles. Hasn't had to take any pain killers en route but does take them overnight to curb any inflammation. Really appreciates the texts and phone calls...."How did they get my mobile number?" I wonder...(blushing)...

Very fussy landlady: "Oh, you've got a bike" "Yes, I did say that when I booked and I did ask if there was secure parking for the bike." "Well, I thought you could just lock it to a post outside" "No". (Not bloody likely – bike cost c£1,500! What's she like?) Finally cajoled landlady into letting him store it in the laundry room overnight and gave Roy the key.

Right, before we move on, some facts on nutrition, I know you're dying to know this stuff. Currently displayed on bed in front of him:

10 brunch bars
9 protein bars
7 energy bars
5 caffeine energy gels
4 energy gels
3 pepperamis
2 chocolate bars
(and a partridge in a pear tree)

Total: about 5,000 calories. This is the 'pocket' food that he's got to eat just to keep moving. (Must have big pockets to fit a tree in. And I bet the partridge is a wriggler.) Roy should eat around 7,000 to 8,000 calories per day so the balance is made up from bacon rolls, pasties, crisps and other snacks on the road. Recovery drink provides 1,200 calories on completion of the day – ideally should be taken within 20 minutes of finishing that day's cycle. Pot Noodle (evening meal) provides 500 calories.

Day Five, Shrewsbury to Taunton (245 km)

Not slept well and didn't want to get up. Very noisy - B&B outside MacDonald's and Pizza Hut. Guests also very noisy using the bathroom (not en-suite). Heard rap music in the night, in sleepy state, thought it was the alarm and started getting up. Then realised that he does not have a radio alarm. And if he did, it would be radio 2, not rap music. Checked clock - only 1:30 am - car pulled up outside blasting out music, so went back to bed.

05:47 *Here we go...*
06:51 *Church Stretton*
07:42 *Ludlow*
08:15 *Dogs would love this place...Wooferton*
09:25 *Nr Hereford - Bacon bap by roadside*
10: 25 Phone call - weeing in a wheat field with poppies...(we've already covered this....) and applying more sudacream (I'm not going to explain where, I'm sure you know) – now getting very sore. Struggled to find water for first part of journey this morning. Road bypasses towns and can add extra mileage to journey. Dearth of burger vans. Has now found one and topped up with water and food. Done about 90km, just come up stonking great hill and about to turn into A466 for Monmouth.

11:18   *Monmouth   ARAF!* (that's Welsh by the way...for stop) Responded with Allez! Allez! Allez! I know it's not Welsh but, hey, it's foreign! What else is a girl meant to say? Anyone know the Welsh for "Go"....

13:11   *Severn Bridge*

14:35   Clifton *Battery low. Switching off (the phone that is...)*

15:23   *Nr Bristol Airport....tempting*

15:30   Phone call – "I'm lost. I mean really lost and have no idea where I am. (This really is becoming a bit of a habit!) I want to be on A38. Now heading out on A370 to Weston Super Mare. Have turned back and now facing East" (It's amazing how he thinks I can locate him from that, but find him I did...) It's that blasted sat nav again...can anyone think of an appropriate name for it? Wallie springs to mind.....Okay, agree route with Roy on map. Turn left onto B3130 and then turn right when hit A38. Called 5 minutes later "Should I have gone immediately right after the semi circle?" "Yes" "Well, I've gone back on myself. Will have to do it again." Clearly mental fatigue is now beginning to make an appearance. Thank goodness there is only 1 day to go. Can't wait until tomorrow. Go Roy!

16:26   *Airport! Extra 20km!*

...and I leave you there on that cliff hanger. Will he make it? Can we wait? More tomorrow....

Day Five, Shrewsbury to Taunton (245 km)

I know you are all perched on the end of your seats wanting to know if he made it last night, so without any further ado, let's continue.....

18:11   *Bridgwater*
19:18   *Here. It has been a long day today – 165 miles,*
        average speed 14.5 miles per hour.

Roy's nicknamed the Sat Nav, "Sat Naff". Mind you, it did redeem itself through Taunton. Roy was too tired to follow his own detailed directions, so set the Sat Nav (sorry Sat naff...) up. Skirted him north of Taunton, then straight through the middle, down some country lanes and brought him out at the exact spot required. Yes, well done! (Although isn't that what sat nav's are meant to do? Bring you out at the exact spot required...) I think this is a bit of a love/hate relationship, don't you? We're going to have watch this...

B&B – very comfortable. Very old and is, well, very old. Roy has a suite this time. One room with double bed, one room with lounge and television for general reclining, another room with toilet and basin, and then a separate room for shower. Sheep skin rug alongside the bed. Views of fields and sheep ...Clothes drying in the window...hmm, that distorts the image a bit. Roy's pushed the boat out tonight and treated himself to an evening meal at the B&B – pasta bake (take that, Pot Noodle...). Hmm, good carbo loading. See, we're getting the hang of this now...Roy v. tired though.

Asked me to check the weather. Wind could be a problem today (no, not that sort of wind...) if it blows in from the west – which it could do being a north westerly - and it seems it will get stronger through the day - 8 mph at 07:00 growing to 15mph towards the end of the day with gusts up to 28mph, which has been the pattern over the last few days. But forecast is dry and sunny with some cloud. Been fairly lucky with the weather all told, and tended to avoid the rain. Has cycled through very wet patches and seen rain on the horizon but hasn't ridden through very much, which is good.

Optimistic about the final day, legs kicked in towards the end of today. (Well, what were they doing before that? I don't know, you just can't rely on some people...I thought he was meant to be a cyclist...Legs are kind of vital to that...aren't they?..)

Day Six (drum roll required), Taunton to Lands End (234 km)

Roy is confident about today. If he maintains same speed as yesterday, he could arrive around 6:00 pm at Lands End (as opposed to the scheduled 8:00 pm). (Buggers up my planning, I tell you...how am I meant to know what time to leave?...) Roughly 15 miles less than Day 5. Have tried to arrange some last minute press coverage, after all this is some achievement, cycling 900 miles without a support car – only a wife at the end of the phone. Hey, I know I'm good but even I have my limitations....

06:00:01   *Once more into the breach.....*(hey, how's that for precision timing, my friends, spot on 6 o' clock, well done Roy....see, practice always makes perfect.....)

06:06   *could have slept all day.....*

06:36   *Devon!* (Welcome home, my man)

07:07   *Willand*

08:56   *Crediton. Really hard today. Looking forward to A30.*

10:10   Widdon Down. Phone call. Slowest day by far – eta at Land's End 9:00 pm. Has met first 25% hill – biggest hill since leaving JOG - up to now, highest was 13%. With weight on the back was really gruelling. (That's the Devon we know and love...just proves the nature of Devon, rolling hills and all that...) Receiving lots of texts – everyone saying "well done and all that", but difficult to keep on top of them. Struggling down little lanes – need both hands going up, going downhill need to maintain speed and concentrate (Shouldn't be trying to read your texts on the move anyway, Roy...Look, mum, no hands...)

Need to sign off now, about to go into a meeting. Will complete blog tomorrow with details on Roy's victorious achievement.

Day Six, continued

Right, where were we my handsomes...

11:58	*Kernow! Last county...country...shame it's so bloody long and thin.....*(In-joke here: the Cornish believe that the Tamar River is 5 miles too short and should have cut Cornwall off completely to become it's own country...)
14:28	Bodmin
15:30	Support car leaves Ivybridge to meet Roy
c16:30	Telecon with Roy – at roundabout signposting Truro and Redruth. ETA: Penzance 18:00/18:30, Lands End 19:00/19:30
c17:00	Meet Roy on A30. Fantastic! Looks very smart in his black and gold Gard & Co. kit. (Which, incidentally, Roy loves...doesn't know how he managed without a gillet before (what a girl!). Apparently, sensitive parts would have been a lot worse off if he had worn some of his existing shorts and padding...) Roy hands over bag from bike, strips off leg warmers and continues. Road very, very busy - dual carriage way: apparently typical of the majority of the journey. Hmmm, don't overly dwell on this....Play leapfrog until Penzance (waiting in lay by's) where support car pulls off for a wee

and refreshment break (no, we are not resorting to farm tracks…). It is impressive the distance Roy can cover in the time and the hills he is taking in his stride…stupid comment I know, bearing in mind he has just cycled 875 miles already, but you know what I mean. The best I can manage is a 10 mile stretch up the Plym Valley – and that usually takes all day with much puffing required.

18:45   Regroup with Roy on A30 on last 4 mile stretch into Land's End, trail him all the way. He is looking comfortable and doing well – and to me, the absolute pro.

c19:00   Arrive at Land's End. Mission accomplished. What a moment!

Okay – let's reflect…

Highs:	Glen Coe on Day Two
Lows:	Cycling into Glasgow on very fast single carriageway in the rain (day two). Cycling up 15% hill between Bickliegh and Crediton (Devon, day six), after completing 25% hills on little gravelly lane (that's Devon for you.)
Fastest speed:	45 miles per hour coming down the hill out of Bodmin. (That's Cornwall for you…) Other high speeds, 42mph coming down Barridale (after Navidale) in Scotland on day one, 42 mph coming down Shap Fell, day three
Time in the saddle:	70 to 80 hours
Why did you do it?:	For the sense achievement.

And that's it, I will leave you there…until next time… (There is a next time?…believe me, he has already started to think about it……)

J x

Other Books

LEJOG Cycling the Google Route

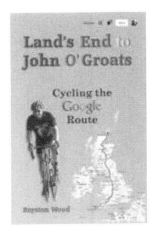

This is a travelogue style account of Royston's second ride across the country.

Smashed from his bicycle by an articulated truck Royston Wood found himself unable to complete a long planned for 875 mile cycling event. Battling the demons of failure he devised a plan to ride a similar distance across the UK from Land's End to John O'Groats. With only a few days to plan the whole trip he delegated the routing to Google Maps. Cycle routing was brand new and in beta testing: what could go wrong...

The book is available as:

Paperback at Amazon
Kindle at Amazon
PDF at www.landsend-to-johnogroats.co.uk

End to End Cycle Route

Also available is Royston's 'Safe' Cycle Route. It is based on the route cycled in LEJOG Cycling the Google Route but with all the bits he moaned about re-routed (and then re-ridden to test it).

It is a set of 18 gpx route files that use quiet roads and lanes, cycle paths, old railway lines and tow paths to guide you from one end of the country to the other. The gpx files are accompanied by a book to tell you how to use and amend them together with lists of accommodation and cycle shops and maps.

The book is available as:

Paperback at Amazon
Kindle at Amazon
PDF at www.landsend-to-johnogroats.co.uk

:
.

13670617R00081

Printed in Great Britain
by Amazon.co.uk, Ltd.,
Marston Gate.